Virtue

D1231448

Virtue

Heather Battaly

polity

First published in 2015 by Polity Press

Polity Press
65 Bridge Street
Cambridge CB2 1UR, UK

Polity Press
350 Main Street
Malden, MA 02148, USA

ISBN-13: 978-0-7456-4953-5
ISBN-13: 978-0-7456-4954-2(pb)

A catalogue record for this book is available from the British Library.

Library of Congress Cataloging-in-Publication Data

Battaly, Heather D., 1969-
  Virtue / Heather D. Battaly.
     pages cm. – (Key Concepts in Philosophy)
  Includes bibliographical references.
  ISBN 978-0-7456-4953-5 (hardcover) – ISBN 978-0-7456-4954-2
(papercover) 1. Virtues. I. Title.
  BJ1521.B38 2014
  179′.9–dc23
                              2014016882

Typeset in 10.5 on 12 pt Sabon
by Toppan Best-set Premedia Limited
Printed and bound in Great Britain by TJ International Ltd, Padstow, Cornwall

For further information on Polity, visit our website: politybooks.com

Contents

Acknowledgments

I am deeply grateful for the support and encouragement of my colleagues, my students, and my friends and family, both inside and outside the discipline of philosophy. I would like to thank Emma Hutchinson, the editor of the Key Concepts in Philosophy Series at Polity, who has been a tremendous source of support. I have greatly benefited from her vision, enthusiasm, patience, and levity. Better editors are not to be had. Several referees for Polity made excellent suggestions about the book proposal for *Virtue*, which shaped the manuscript. I am grateful for their thoughts. Two referees read the manuscript in full. I am deeply indebted to them for their time and effort, their terrific comments, and their support of this project.

Chapter 1 benefited from the brilliant comments of the participants in the Intellectual Virtues and Education Project Seminar at Loyola Marymount University (2012). I am especially grateful to Jason Baehr; and to Mindy Beier, Karen Bohlin, Kate Elgin, Steve Porter, Ron Ritchhart, Wayne Riggs, Emily Robertson, Stephen Sherblom, and Harvey Siegel. Thank you all for your comments and encouragement.

My colleagues and students at Cal State Fullerton have been wonderfully supportive. Special thanks to my colleagues Merrill Ring and Craig Ihara, and my students Nahal Bahri and Martha Matlock, all of whom sent me comments on chapters. I am also thankful to Cal State Fullerton for supporting this project with a grant and a sabbatical leave. In addition, I am honored to have received a grant from the Spencer Foundation's Initiative on Philosophy in Educational Policy and Practice (2011), which supported research on Chapter 7.

I am deeply grateful to my philosophical heroes: Neera Badhwar, Kate Elgin, Christine Swanton, Liezl van Zyl, and especially Linda Zagzebski. Thank you for your conversations and comments on chapters, your enthusiasm and support, and your general awesomeness. My debt to Linda is especially deep. She has helped to form my identity as a philosopher, and I feel privileged and lucky to count her among my philosophical family. I am also indebted to my philosophical siblings – Amy Coplan, Jason Baehr, and Wayne Riggs – who are constant sources of inspiration, admiration, and encouragement. I continue to learn from their work and their ways of doing philosophy. It has been an honor to grow up in the discipline alongside the three of them. William Alston and Michael Stocker, my mentors in graduate school, have shaped the kind of philosophy that I do, and the way that I do it. Here, no amount, degree, or sort of gratitude is enough. My hope is that this book does philosophy in a way that would make them proud.

Finally, I am grateful for encouragement from my friends and family. Thank you for taking pride in what I do. Thanks especially to Jessica Klingsberg and Katie Kruse, who shared their thoughts about Chapter 4. My deepest thanks go to Clifford Roth, who read every line of the book, served as a sounding board for examples, and who has made it possible for me to flourish as a philosopher, and as a human being, in so many ways. I am lucky to have him in my life.

For Clifford Samuel Roth, with love, admiration, and gratitude

1
What Are the Virtues?

1.1 A Working Definition of Virtue

What is a virtue, and how are virtues different from vices? To get started on a definition of virtue, let's think about the people we know well – our friends. Which of their qualities count as virtues? What qualities do they have – not just as friends, but as people in general – that we would classify as obvious examples of virtues?

We might reasonably reply that our friends are, for instance: honest, smart, fair, dependable, brave, generous, open-minded, or funny. Or that they: enjoy life, do not give up easily, care about others, stand up for themselves and others, have good judgment, offer good advice, or know when others are upset and how to make them feel better. Philosophers have, at one time or another, counted all these qualities as virtues. Several of these qualities – courage (bravery), justice (fairness), temperance (enjoying life), and wisdom (which is connected to having good judgment and giving good advice) – are widely thought to be virtues. They appear on the lists of virtues generated by ancient philosophers, like Plato and Aristotle, early modern philosophers, like David Hume, and contemporary philosophers, like Rosalind Hursthouse and Linda Zagzebski. Other qualities – like wit (being funny) – appear on some lists (Aristotle's and Hume's), but not others. Likewise, being open-minded appears on some lists (Zagzebski's), but not others. Any initial definition of virtue – one whose primary job is to distinguish virtue from vice – should be broad enough to include all of the above qualities. Finer distinctions among different sorts of virtues can be made after we have generated a working definition of virtue in general.

Since we do not know one another's friends, let's examine some familiar illustrations of four of the above qualities: being smart, empathy (which is connected to caring about others and knowing when they are upset), open-mindedness, and courage.

First, Hermione Granger, one of the characters in J. K. Rowling's *Harry Potter* series, is by all accounts *smart*. Hermione is smart in the sense that she knows a pile of facts, in her case "facts" about spells and the history of magic. But more importantly for present purposes, she is also smart in the sense that she has reliable intellectual capacities and skills. For instance, she has an excellent memory, and is skilled at logical problem solving. Hermione is so good at remembering magical facts that she annoys her classmates (whose memories are not as good) and even some of her teachers (who grow tired of calling on her). Hermione's memory contributes to her success as a student – she scores high marks on her exams. Outside the classroom, her memory saves her friends' lives on more than one occasion. For example, in *Harry Potter and the Sorcerer's Stone*, Hermione saves Ron Weasley by remembering which spell to use against Devil's Snare. Hermione uses her skills in logic to figure out that the creature guarding the chamber of secrets is a basilisk (*Harry Potter and the Chamber of Secrets*) and that Professor Lupin is a werewolf (*Harry Potter and the Prisoner of Azkaban*). Qualities like reliable memory and logical skills are featured on Ernest Sosa's list of intellectual virtues. According to Sosa, these qualities count as virtues because they reliably produce true beliefs. Sosa's theory is addressed in Chapter 2.

Second, television character Deanna Troi, therapist to the crew of the *Enterprise* on *Star Trek: The Next Generation* (1987–94), is clearly *empathic*. She excels at knowing others' emotions: for instance, she knows when others are upset, happy, angry, afraid, despairing, or in love. As a member of a species of "empaths" (Troi is part Betazoid), she has the ability to directly feel what others in the vicinity are feeling. Her empathic ability to detect the emotions of aliens extricates the *Enterprise* from several dangerous situations, and proves vital in diplomatic negotiations. Troi can also feel the emotions of the *Enterprise* crew as a whole (she can gauge the overall mood of the crew), and can detect specific emotions in individual crew members. For example, she recognizes that Dr. Beverly Crusher is in love ("The Host"), and that Captain Jean-Luc Picard is grieving (*Generations*, 1994), though each emotion is meant to be secret. Troi even uses her empathic abilities to discover and solve a murder ("Eye of the Beholder"). She also cares about her crewmates, and counsels them through their troubles – she knows how to make them feel better, and get better. Of course, we do not have the advantages of Troi's Betazoid physiology – her empathic abilities far exceed our own. But we do still succeed in sharing the emotions of others and caring about their well-being. In contrast with Troi, this sometimes requires effort on our part: we must actively imagine the emotions of a person who is a different gender or race, or who lives in a culture that is different from our own – their emotions do not simply pop into our heads. Our ability to empathize likely relies both on our voluntary efforts to take another person's perspective, and on our hard-wired capacities for mimicking and mirroring others. Empathy plays a central role in Michael Slote's virtue ethics. Slote thinks that qualities like empathy and empathic caring count as virtues because they involve morally valuable motives. Slote's theory is addressed in Chapter 3.

Third, Dr. Gregory House, protagonist of the medical drama *House M.D.* (Fox, 2004–12), is clearly a brilliant diagnostician – he reliably succeeds in diagnosing patients whom no one else can diagnose. He is also a spectacular misanthrope. He is frequently cruel to his patients and colleagues, and often lies to get what he wants. House is neither caring, honest, just, nor temperate (he is addicted to Vicodin). But, arguably, he is *open-minded*. In nearly every episode, House elicits possible diagnoses from his team, and considers whether those diagnoses are true. He is simultaneously alive to the possibility that his own diagnoses might be false. To illustrate: in "Occam's Razor" (2004), House and his team consider multiple conditions that their patient might have, including: a viral heart infection (Dr. Foreman), a carcinoid tumor (Dr. Chase), an allergy (Dr. Cameron), and a combination of sinusitis and hypothyroidism (Dr. House). When all of their hypotheses – including his own – are proven false, House considers yet another alternative: that the patient, whose first symptom was coughing, accidentally received the wrong medication for his cough. (The team discovers that House is correct – the patient was given gout medication, which caused the rest of his symptoms.) Considering alternative hypotheses helps House get to the truth. In fact, House is so dependent on this process that when his team quits, he relies on other people – like the hospital's janitor – to help him evaluate alternative diagnoses and solve his case. House also cares about the truth. He is not motivated by money or fame, or even because he cares about his patients; he doesn't. He only cares about one thing: getting the truth. Dr. House is clearly not morally virtuous. But, given that it is possible to have some virtues but not others, House is not precluded from being open-minded. Open-mindedness is one of the key intellectual virtues identified by Linda Zagzebski. She argues that open-mindedness is a virtue both because it reliably produces true beliefs and because it involves a valuable motivation for truth. Zagzebski's view is addressed in Chapter 3.

Fourth, Alice Paul (1885–1977) fought for and helped to achieve women's suffrage in the United States, and (to a lesser extent) in Britain. In both the US and Britain, Paul risked her health, and even her life, to get women the right to vote. Though it is more difficult to identify virtues in real people than in fictional characters, Alice Paul had the virtue of *courage* if anyone did. As the leader of the Congressional Union of the National American Woman Suffrage Association, and founder of the National Woman's Party (NWP), Paul fought for and attained an amendment to the US Constitution that guaranteed women the right to vote. This achievement came at great risk. Paul argued for suffrage in speeches and in writing, organized and marched in suffrage parades, and picketed the Woodrow Wilson White House.[1] Suffragist speakers and marchers were subject to verbal derision and physical threats. White House picketers, who carried banners but were otherwise silent, were attacked by mobs and arrested for obstructing traffic. Paul, and other suffragists, continued picketing the White House even though they knew that they were risking physical harm, arrest, and jail-time. During the Fall of 1917, 168 suffragists were imprisoned, choosing to serve jail-time rather than pay fines (Adams and Keene 2008: 173). In October 1917, Paul was sentenced to seven months in jail. While in prison, she went on a hunger strike in order to demonstrate that she was willing to risk her health and life for suffrage. As a result of her disobedience, she was placed in solitary confinement, threatened with institutionalization, and physically restrained and force-fed. She did not give up: she continued her hunger strike until she was released from prison in November 1917. Less than two years later, the US Congress passed the 19th Amendment. Paul faced dangers, stood up for herself and others, and did so not for the sake of fame but because she believed that women should have the right to vote. Due in good part to the courage of Alice Paul and other suffragists like her, women in the US and the United Kingdom have been enfranchised for nearly 100 years. Courage is widely counted as a virtue, appearing on the lists of many philosophers, including Aristotle. Aristotle argues that courageous people face dangers that are worthwhile, and do so because of good motives. Arguably, he thinks that courage is a virtue because it both attains good ends or effects, and involves valuable motivations. Aristotle's account of the virtues is addressed in Chapter 3.

The qualities in the above examples are diverse. Some are (largely) hard-wired capacities, like reliable memory. Others are acquired skills, like the ability to solve logical puzzles. Still others are acquired character traits, like empathy, open-mindedness, and courage. So, what makes all of these qualities, and the other qualities we attributed to our friends, virtues? The answer is that they all make us better people. *Virtues are qualities that make one an excellent person.* A person can be excellent in a variety of ways: she can be excellent insofar as she has a good memory, or insofar as she is skilled at logical problem solving, or insofar as she is open-minded, just, or benevolent. In short, virtues are excellences.[2]

In contrast, vices are defects. *Vices are qualities that make us worse people.* Analogously, a person can be defective in a variety of ways: she can be defective insofar as she has a bad memory, or insofar as she lacks logical skills, or insofar as she is dogmatic, unjust, or cruel. It is important to note that according to these working definitions, virtues are qualities that make us excellent as people in general, rather than merely excellent in some specific occupation or role. Likewise, vices make us worse as people in general, rather than merely worse at some specific occupation or role. We do not all share the same occupations or roles – some of us are parents, others are not; some of us are teachers, others are students, still others are CEOs. But we are all people. Accordingly, the virtues and vices in these working definitions pertain to all of us, no matter what our specific jobs or roles. Sometimes the qualities that make us better at some specific occupation or role overlap with the qualities that make us better people in general. For instance, empathy arguably makes us better parents, teachers, and doctors; and also makes us better people. But these qualities do not always overlap. In fact, sometimes the qualities that make us better at a specific occupation or role make us worse as people in general. To illustrate: dishonesty arguably makes one better in the role of police interrogator, but it makes one worse as a person in general. (Jane Tennison, protagonist of the television series *Prime Suspect* [ITV, 1991–2006], is a superb interrogator partly because she misleads and manipulates the people she interviews.) Since dishonesty makes one worse as a person in general, it is a vice, not a virtue. Likewise, honesty arguably makes one worse as an interrogator, but better as a person in general. Accordingly, honesty is a virtue, not a vice.

These working definitions of virtue and vice are broad. They include moral qualities – like benevolence and cruelty – but they also include intellectual qualities – like open-mindedness and dogmatism. They include qualities over whose acquisition we exercise considerable control, and for which we can clearly be praised (e.g., courage) or blamed (e.g., cowardice). But they also include qualities over which we exercise little control – like reliable memory – qualities which we find ourselves either with or without, due to no merit or fault of our own. David Hume famously includes all of these sorts of qualities – intellectual as well as moral, and involuntary as well as voluntary – on his lists of virtues and vices. In his *Enquiry Concerning the Principles of Morals*, Hume argues that attempts to exclude intellectual qualities from the category of virtues will fail. For instance, he claims that if we were to "lay hold of the distinction between intellectual and moral endowments, and affirm the last alone to be real and genuine virtues, because they alone [led] to action" then we would quickly discover that "many of those qualities . . . called intellectual virtues, such as prudence, penetration, discernment, discretion, [have] also a considerable influence on conduct" (1966/1751: 156). In short, Hume's point is that intellectual virtues are no less real or genuine than moral virtues. In his *Treatise of Human Nature*, Hume argues that involuntary abilities cannot be excluded from the category of virtues, since some of them are "useful" to the people who have them; that is, some involuntary abilities enable the people who have them to attain good effects (1978/1738: 610). Accordingly, he thinks that virtues that are involuntary are no less real than virtues that are voluntary. Our working definitions agree with Hume on both these points. It is also worth noting that our working definitions are broad enough to be compatible with both theism and atheism – one need not be a theist to endorse our working definitions of virtue or vice. Here, too, they agree with Hume.[3]

In fact, our working definitions of virtue and vice are so broad that, as they stand, they are difficult to apply. To apply them, we need to be able to determine whether a quality is an excellence or a defect, and why it makes one a better person or a worse person. With this end in mind, we can distinguish between two key concepts of virtue, both of which are compatible with, but less vague than, our working definition of virtue.

1.2 Two Key Concepts of Virtue

Different qualities can make one a better person in different ways. The historical and contemporary literature on virtue emphasizes two key ways in which a quality can make one a better person. First, a quality might enable one to reliably attain good ends or effects – like true beliefs, or the welfare of others. These goods are often external to us. Second, a quality might involve good motives – like caring about truths, or about the welfare of others. Motives are internal to us. According to the first key concept, reliable success in attaining good ends or effects is what makes a quality a virtue. To be virtuous, one need only be reliably successful at attaining good ends or effects – at producing external goods. So, if a venture capitalist reliably succeeds in helping others by donating money to a hospital, then he is (to that extent) virtuous. But according to the second key concept, being consistently successful at attaining good ends or effects is not enough, and might not even be required, for virtue. What is required, and what makes a quality a virtue, are good motives, which are internal. So, if the venture capitalist reliably succeeds in helping others but his motives are selfish – he donates money because he wants to get his name on a building or get tax write-offs – then he is not virtuous.[4]

1.2.1 Ends Matter: Virtues Attain Good Ends or Effects

According to the *first key concept of virtue*, what makes a quality a virtue, as opposed to a vice, is its success in attaining good ends or effects, many of which are external to us. This success need not be perfect, but it must be reliable. Hence, qualities that rarely, but occasionally, fail to attain good ends or effects can still be virtues; but qualities that *reliably* fail to attain good ends or effects cannot. This means that people who try, but consistently fail, to help others (like the character Mr. Bean) do not have the virtue of benevolence. They may want to help others – they may have good motives – but if they consistently bungle the job, they are not virtuous. Likewise, people who try, but consistently fail, to get true beliefs do not have intellectual virtues. They may want to get truths – they may have good motives – but if they consistently botch the job, they are not virtuous either. According to this concept, bad luck can prevent us from having virtues. People who have the bad luck of being in a demon-world, in which all their beliefs turn out to be false, or in an oppressive society, in which all or most of their actions turn out to produce harm, do not have virtues. In other words, reliably attaining good ends or effects is necessary for a quality to be a virtue.

Reliably attaining good ends or effects is also sufficient for a quality to be a virtue. Philosophers who endorse this concept argue that since good ends or effects are what matters (since good ends or effects are valuable), any quality that reliably succeeds in getting good ends or effects will also be valuable – it will be a virtue. This means that any quality – whether it is a natural capacity, an acquired skill, or an acquired character trait – will count as a virtue as long as it consistently produces good ends or effects. Accordingly, venture capitalists who consistently succeed in helping others via charitable donations have the virtue of benevolence, even if they do not care about others and are solely motivated by fame or tax write-offs. Likewise, students who reliably arrive at true beliefs as a result of their logical skills have intellectual virtues, even if they do not care about truth and are solely motivated to get good grades or make money (some websites pay students to get good grades). In short, one need only be successful at getting good ends or effects to be virtuous; one need not have good motives.[5] Getting good ends or effects is the only thing that matters for virtue.

Are the virtues intrinsically, constitutively, or instrumentally valuable?

According to the first key concept, good ends or effects are what matter – they are intrinsically valuable. In other words, they are valuable for their *own* sakes – they are valuable even if they do not produce, or are not part of, anything else of value. It is notoriously difficult to determine what (if any-thing) has *intrinsic* value, but health, true beliefs, knowledge, and the well-being of oneself and others have all been top candidates. In contrast, something has *instrumental* value if it is valuable as a means to producing *something else* of value. For instance, medication is valuable as a means to producing health, but not valuable for its own sake – if it failed to produce health, it would not be valuable. Finally, something has *constitutive* value if it is *part* of something that is valuable. For instance, the piece of oilcloth in Picasso's 1912 collage, *Still Life with Chair Caning*, is valuable because it is part of the (presumably) valuable collage. The piece of oilcloth is not valuable for its own sake, nor is it instrumentally valuable in this case since it does not produce the collage; rather, it is valuable because it is part of the collage.

These examples demonstrate that some things, like medication, are only valuable in one of the above ways. Medication is only instrumentally valuable; it is neither intrinsically nor constitutively valuable. But, this does not mean that all things are only valuable in one of the above ways. These three sorts of value do not necessarily exclude one another. Hence, it is possible that some things – like friendship – are valuable in more than one of these ways, or even in all three ways. Friendship might be (intrinsically) valuable for its own sake, (instrumentally) valuable because it produces something else of value like joy, and (constitutively) valuable because it is part of something that is valuable like living a good life.

Philosophers who defend this first key concept of virtue argue that the virtues are either instrumentally or constitutively valuable (or both). The virtues will be instrumentally valuable if they produce good ends – if they produce something of intrinsic value, like well-being or true beliefs. The virtues will be constitutively valuable if they are part of a good end – if they are part of something that is intrinsically valuable, like living a good life. In contrast, philosophers who defend the second key concept think that the virtues are intrinsically valuable (see section 1.2.2).

Are the virtues teleological or nonteleological?

Philosophers who endorse the first key concept all agree that good ends or effects are intrinsically valuable. But some of them focus on ends; others on effects. So, this first key concept of virtue comes in two different varieties: a teleological variety that focuses on ends, and a nonteleological variety that focuses on effects. Generally speaking, *teleology* is the view that things and people have built-in *ends* or functions.

For instance, Plato and Aristotle argue that eyes, knives, workhorses, sculptors, and people in general all have such ends or functions. They argue that the function (end) of an eye is to see, of a knife is to cut, of a workhorse is to haul, and of a sculptor is to sculpt. Of course, determining the function (end) of a person in general is no easy task. Each of these functions – seeing, cutting, etc. – can be performed well or poorly. According to the teleological variety of our first key concept, virtues are whatever qualities enable a thing or person to perform its function well (to attain its end), and vices are whatever qualities explain why a thing or person is performing its function poorly (failing to attain its end). In Plato's words, "anything that has a function performs it well by means of its own . . . virtue, and badly by means of its vice" (*Republic*, Book I: 353c). Hence, the sharpness of a knife is one of its virtues since sharpness is responsible for its cutting well (attaining its end); the dullness of a knife is one of its vices since dullness is responsible for its cutting poorly (failing to attain its end). Analogously, the virtues and vices of a person will be whatever qualities are responsible for her performing her function well or poorly – for her success or failure in attaining her end. It then follows that to figure out which of our qualities are virtues – which of our qualities makes us better as people – we must figure out the function or end of a person. This function or end is meant to be intrinsically valuable.

Other philosophers reject the teleological variety of this concept. They doubt that things and people have built-in ends or functions. Instead, they provide an analysis of virtue that makes no mention of function. They define virtues and vices in terms of *effects*. Accordingly, a quality will count as a virtue if it consistently produces good effects. A quality will count as a vice if it consistently fails to produce good effects. Of course, the challenge for this variety of our first key concept is to figure out which effects are good – which are intrinsically valuable.

It should be noted that, in actual practice, it can be difficult to tell these two varieties of our first key concept apart. This is because they often end up agreeing about which ends, or effects, are good. For instance, both varieties standardly conclude that true beliefs and the welfare of others count among good ends or effects. When this happens, the difference between the two varieties amounts to a theoretical one – they agree in practice about which things count as good, but they disagree about why those things count as good. Arguably, the teleological variety has an extra step in its explanation: it ties intrinsic value to ends and functions; the nonteleological variety does not.

Preview of four theorists: Plato, Aristotle, Sosa, Driver

Each of the four theorists addressed in Chapter 2 – Plato, Aristotle, Ernest Sosa, and Julia Driver – employs the first key concept of virtue. Plato, Aristotle, and, to a lesser extent, Sosa endorse the teleological variety. Driver endorses the nonteleological variety. All four theorists think that the virtues are instrumentally valuable. (The distinctions above can cross-cut one another.) Arguably, Plato, Aristotle, and Sosa think that the virtues are also constitutively valuable. Let's begin with a preview of Plato's view.

Plato is famous for defining virtues teleologically – in terms of functions or ends. In *Republic*, he argues that the function of a person includes deliberating, ruling oneself, and, more broadly, living. He contends that virtues are qualities that enable a person to perform these functions well. In other words, he thinks that the virtues are qualities that enable us to deliberate well, rule ourselves well, and thereby live well.

Which qualities are these? To identify the virtues, Plato argues that each person has a soul that is divided into three parts – reason, spirit, and appetite. Each of these parts has its own particular function. Roughly, the function (end) of reason is to rule the soul and to know what is good for the whole person, including knowing which things she should fear, and which things she should desire.[6] The function (end) of spirit is to enforce what reason says about which things should be feared; the function (end) of appetite is to accept what reason says about which things should be desired. Each of these functions can be performed well or poorly. Plato thinks that when one's reason, spirit, and appetite are all functioning well, one knows what is good and one puts this knowledge into practice – one fears all and only the things one should (to use contemporary examples, one fears combat but not mice), and desires all and only the things one should (one desires sex, but not sex with one's best friend's partner). On his view, the virtue of wisdom is what enables reason to function well, since the wise person knows what is good and deliberates well. Likewise, courage is what enables spirit to function well, since the courageous person fears what he should; and temperance is what enables appetite to function well, since the temperate person desires what he should. The virtue of justice is what enables the whole person to function well, and function without internal conflict – justice enables each part of the soul to do "its own work," in harmony with the other parts (*Republic*, Book IV: 441d–e). Hence, justice, in concert with the other virtues, enables a person to deliberate well, rule herself well, and thereby live well. Arguably, Plato thinks that the virtues are instrumentally valuable – because they enable us to live well; and constitutively valuable – since being virtuous is part of what it is to live well.

As a student of Plato's, *Aristotle* inherited the first key concept of virtue from him. Aristotle makes use of the teleological variety of this concept in Books I and VI of his *Nicomachean Ethics* (NE). (But he makes use of the second key concept of virtue in much of the rest of NE.) Let's begin with Book VI of the *Nicomachean Ethics*. The goal of NE.VI is to explain the intellectual virtues. Here, Aristotle takes several cues from Plato. Like Plato, Aristotle thinks that there is a rational part of the soul, and that wisdom is what enables it to function well, since wisdom gets us knowledge. But, unlike Plato, Aristotle thinks that there are two types of wisdom and two types of knowledge. According to Aristotle, the rational part of the soul is itself subdivided into two further parts – the contemplative part and the calculative part. The function (end) of the contemplative part is to get theoretical knowledge, which, for Aristotle, included truths about geometry (e.g., every triangle has three sides). The function (end) of the calculative part is to get practical knowledge, like which action one should perform (e.g., I should finish the presentation that is due tomorrow instead of drinking lots of gin). Aristotle uses these functions to identify different virtues. He argues: "The work of both the intellectual parts . . . is truth. Therefore the states that are most strictly those in respect of which each of these parts will reach truth are the virtues of the two parts" (NE.1139b11–13). In other words, intellectual virtues are qualities that enable us to perform these functions well – they enable us to reliably attain practical or theoretical knowledge, respectively. Aristotle contends that practical wisdom (*phronesis*) and skill (*techne*) are the virtues of the calculative part – they get us practical truths and knowledge; while philosophical wisdom (*sophia*), intuitive reason (*nous*), and scientific knowledge (*episteme*) are the virtues of the contemplative part – they get us theoretical truths and knowledge. Arguably, in NE.VI, Aristotle is thinking of the intellectual virtues as instrumentally valuable – valuable because they produce knowledge, which is itself intrinsically valuable.

In Book I of the *Nicomachean Ethics*, Aristotle defines virtues, and the good life, in terms of functions. The overarching goal of NE.I is to define human flourishing (*eudaimonia*), or the good life. Aristotle contends that, contrary to popular belief, the good life does not consist solely in pleasure or wealth. Instead, he defines the good life in terms of the function (end) of a human being. He argues that the function of a human being is, roughly, rational activity. Rational activity is what makes us distinctive. Aristotle's notion of rational activity is broader than it might initially seem. It includes contemplating theories and calculating which actions to perform. But we also engage in rational activity when our appetites obey reason – when we fear, desire, and do what reason tells us. Of course, it is possible for us to perform our function as humans (rational activity) well or poorly. Here, as in NE.VI, Aristotle assumes that to perform any function well one must have the corresponding virtues. Accordingly, he identifies courage, temperance, justice, practical wisdom, and philosophical wisdom as virtues, since they all enable us to excel at rational activity. Aristotle concludes that since the good life consists in performing our function as humans (rational activity) well, and since virtues are what enable us to perform this function well (to excel at rational activity), the good life consists in virtuous rational activity. Arguably, in NE.I, Aristotle is thinking of the virtues as being both instrumentally and constitutively valuable: valuable both because they enable us to excel at rational activity, and because virtuous rational activity is itself part of the good life (which is intrinsically valuable).

It should be noted that though both Plato and Aristotle think that we must have good desires or motives in order to be morally virtuous, this is here purely a result of the rich notion of human function that they endorse. If they are correct – if virtues are whatever qualities enable us to excel at rational activity, excel at ruling ourselves, and excel at living in general – then it is no wonder that virtues require internal features like good desires and motives. If human function is partly internal, then we can expect the virtues to be partly internal. But if we instead endorse more modest ends or effects – like the external production of true beliefs or well-being – then we can expect motives to drop out of the picture. Sosa's and Driver's views each illustrate this point. Neither of them thinks that good motives are required for the virtues. In sum, there is nothing about the first key concept of virtue itself that forces virtues to require good motives. According to the first key concept, it is getting good ends that matters for virtue. If good motives end up being required, this is purely because of one's choice of an internal end.

Ernest Sosa, a contemporary epistemologist, applies the first key concept to intellectual virtues, like reliable memory and vision. Sosa straddles both varieties of the first key concept. When endorsing the teleological variety, he argues that "grasping the truth about one's environment" is one of the "proper ends of a human being" (1991: 271). So, like Plato and Aristotle, he thinks that one of our main functions as people is to get true beliefs. Sosa also uses Plato's *Republic*, and Book VI of Aristotle's *Nicomachean Ethics*, to argue that "there is a . . . sense of 'virtue' . . . in which anything with a function – natural or artificial – does have virtues" (1991: 271). Accordingly, Sosa construes the intellectual virtues as qualities that enable a person to perform her function of getting truths well. A person performs this function well when she reliably gets true beliefs – when she gets more true beliefs than false ones. A person performs this function poorly when she is unreliable – when she gets more false beliefs than true ones. Hence, Sosa thinks that intellectual virtues are whatever qualities reliably get us true beliefs.

Elsewhere, Sosa arrives at the same conclusion, but does so via the nonteleological variety of the first key concept. For instance, in "The Place of Truth in Epistemology," Sosa argues that even if teleology fails – even if it is ultimately implausible to ascribe functions to human beings – true beliefs will still be good. Why are true beliefs good? Sosa skips the extra step of tying intrinsic value to function, and instead argues that true beliefs are themselves intrinsically valuable.[7]

It is important to note that whichever of the first key concept he employs, Sosa draws the same conclusions. He thinks that intellectual virtues are whatever qualities enable us to consistently get more true beliefs than false ones. Getting good ends or effects – true beliefs – is what matters for intellectual virtue; neither good motives nor good actions are required. Accordingly, intellectual virtues are at least instrumentally valuable – they are valuable as a means to producing true beliefs. On Sosa's view, hard-wired capacities (like memory, vision, induction, deduction, and introspection) and acquired skills (like doing proofs in logic, or reading MRI films) are paradigmatic intellectual virtues when they are reliable, and paradigmatic intellectual vices when they are unreliable.[8] Reliable vision, memory, etc. count as virtues even though they aren't perfect. Our memories are hardly perfect – even Hermione's isn't. They sometimes produce false beliefs about historical dates, phone numbers, addresses, etc. But a quality need not be infallible to be an intellectual virtue – it need not always produce true beliefs. It need only produce more true beliefs than false ones; it must be likely to produce a true belief. So, as long as one's memory produces more true beliefs than false ones, it is a virtue. If, on the other hand, one's memory is unreliable – if it is likely to produce a false belief – then it is an intellectual vice.

Julia Driver, a contemporary ethicist, applies the first key concept to moral virtues. She endorses the nonteleological variety of the first key concept. In *Uneasy Virtue*, she argues that virtues are qualities that consistently produce good effects, and vices are qualities that consistently produce bad effects. In her words, moral virtues are "character traits that systematically produce more actual good than not" (2001: 68). Like Sosa, Driver thinks that a quality need not be perfect to count as a virtue. Thus, she argues that justice and benevolence are virtues because they are highly likely to produce good effects, even though they occasionally fail to do so. Likewise, maliciousness is a vice because it is highly likely to produce bad effects, even though it occasionally fails to do so. Driver explicitly contends that good effects are the only things that matter for virtue – good motives are neither necessary nor sufficient for virtue. On her view, good motives are not necessary because if one consistently produces good effects, then one has virtues, even if one's motives are bad. Accordingly, the venture capitalist who consistently donates to hospitals has the virtue of benevolence, even though his motives are selfish. Good motives are not sufficient because people who consistently produce bad effects do not have virtues, even if they are well intentioned. Accordingly, the bungler who produces more harm than good lacks benevolence, despite his good motives.

In short, Driver thinks that external effects are all that matter. On her view, which effects are good, and why? Driver argues that there are multiple sorts of good effects, including true beliefs, the well-being of others, and our own well-being (2001: 102–103). Why are these things good? Driver takes a strong stand against teleological views of the good, explicitly arguing that we should not define the good in terms of function. Instead, she argues that true beliefs and well-being are good for their own sakes; and that the virtues are instrumentally valuable because they produce goods like true beliefs and well-being.

1.2.2 Motives Matter: Virtues Require Good Motives

The first key concept of virtue maintains that attaining good ends or effects – like true beliefs, the well-being of others – is the only thing that matters for virtue. As long as one consistently attains good ends or effects, one is virtuous. In contrast, the second key concept maintains that attaining goods is either not enough, or is not even required, for virtue. It also matters *why* one attains, or tries to attain, those goods – good motives also matter. After all, one might do volunteer work or donate money to charity for entirely selfish reasons – not because one cares about the people who are helped, but because one cares solely about one's own image or about making *oneself* feel better. To illustrate, a column in *The Fullerton Observer*, a local newspaper in Fullerton, California, argues that we should help others because "helping others makes us feel good." It encourages us to "do something very selfish today: help someone else!" According to the second key concept, people who follow this advice are not virtuous, even if they consistently succeed in helping others. They are not virtuous, because they lack good motives. The same can be said of students who reliably arrive at true beliefs, not because they care about truth, but solely because they want to get good grades or make money.

Unlike the first key concept, the second key concept maintains that good motives are necessary for a quality to be a virtue. Why would good motives be necessary if one was already reliably producing good effects? Those who endorse the second key concept have two reasons for thinking that good motives are necessary for virtues. First, they think virtues are praiseworthy, and that praise and blame should only be attached to things we can control. To illustrate, I shouldn't blame a person for her unreliable eyesight, or praise her for her reliable eyesight, since she has no control over the natural capacities she ends up with. To be praiseworthy, virtues must be (to a considerable extent) under our control. And, arguably, we have greater (though not complete) control over our motives and actions than we do over our effects in the world. If our motives are developed over time via practice and effort, then we have considerable control over whether we end up caring about helping others, or only about making ourselves feel better. But, we have less control over our effects in the world, since our good intentions can be defeated by bad luck. Due to no fault of our own, our donations to charitable organizations can end up in the hands of dictators instead of the people who need help.[9] As the Scottish poet Robert Burns wrote in *To a Mouse*: "the best laid schemes of mice and men go often askew." In short, virtues require good motives and good actions because, without them, virtues would not be praiseworthy.

Second, these philosophers think that the virtues tell us who we are as individual people; they reveal what we care about and value. Accordingly, good motives are necessary for virtue because they tell us what we care about, and do so in ways that good actions and natural capacities can't. Good actions are limited in what they can tell us about character. Two people may both consistently donate to charity; but one may donate solely to advance his own reputation, while the other donates to help those in need. Natural capacities (reliable eyesight) are even more limited, since children and animals can have these capacities even though they have not yet, and may never, develop any values to speak of. For both of the above reasons, the second key concept restricts virtues to acquired qualities; whereas the first key concept allows for both natural and acquired qualities.

Are good motives enough for virtue, or do virtues also require attaining good ends or effects?

According to the second key concept, good motives matter – they are required for virtue. Are good motives, combined with good actions, enough for virtue? For instance, is consistently caring about the well-being of others and doing what a benevolent person would do enough for the virtue of benevolence? Or is something else also needed? Some advocates of the second key concept argue that we also need to reliably get good ends or effects. Others disagree, arguing that good motives and good actions are sufficient. Consequently, this key concept also comes in two varieties: the motives-actions-and-ends variety; and the motives-actions-no-ends variety.

According to the *motives-actions-and-ends* variety, to be virtuous, one must have good motives, perform good actions, and be reliably successful at producing external goods. So, to have the virtue of benevolence, one must consistently care about the well-being of others, consistently do what a benevolent person would do, and consistently succeed in improving the welfare of others. If one cares about and tries to help others, but one's efforts go astray due to bad luck, then one does not have the virtue of benevolence. Likewise, if one cares about and tries to get truths, but has the bad luck of being in a deceptive environment, one does not have intellectual virtues. To have virtues, one must be effective. Good intentions and good actions are not enough for virtue; getting external goods still matters.

In contrast, according to the *motives-actions-no-ends variety*, having good motives and performing good actions are required for being virtuous, but getting external goods is not. What matters is whether one consistently wants and tries to get external goods. Suppose one consistently tries one's best to get truths, but due to no fault of one's own has the bad luck of being in surroundings that are deceptive; or tries one's best to help others by donating to charity, but due to no fault of one's own has the bad luck of picking a charity whose shipment of food is stolen. Arguably, this bad luck does not detract from the agent's character, since (presumably) she could not have foreseen it, and cannot be blamed for it. Similarly, we would not blame paramedics who do whatever they can to help accident victims, but fail to save them because of the severity of the accident. According to this variety of the second key concept, external success is not required for virtue.

Are the virtues intrinsically, constitutively, or instrumentally valuable?

Philosophers who endorse the second key concept either defend the motives-actions-and-ends variety or the motives-actions-no-ends variety. Those who defend the motives-actions-and-ends variety typically think that the virtues are valuable in all three ways. The virtues are intrinsically valuable because they require good motives, and good motives are valuable for their own sakes. The virtues are constitutively valuable insofar as they are part of living well or flourishing (which is itself intrinsically valuable). Finally, they think the virtues are instrumentally valuable because the virtues also require reliably getting good ends or effects, like well-being and truth (which are also intrinsically valuable). In contrast, philosophers who defend the motives-actions-no-ends variety do not think that reliably getting external goods is required for virtue. Accordingly, they argue that the virtues need not be instrumentally valuable, but are intrinsically and constitutively valuable.

Preview of five theorists: Aristotle, Hursthouse, Zagzebski, Montmarquet, Slote

Each of the five theorists addressed in Chapter 3 – Aristotle, Rosalind Hursthouse, Linda Zagzebski, James Montmarquet, and Michael Slote – employs the second key concept of virtue. Zagzebski endorses the motives-actions-and-ends variety. Slote and Montmarquet endorse the motives-actions-no-ends variety. Aristotle and Hursthouse are standardly taken to fall in the former camp, but this may depend on how we interpret them. Let's begin with Aristotle.

Though *Aristotle* employs the first key concept of virtue in Books I and VI of *Nicomachean Ethics*, he employs the second key concept in the remainder of NE. In Book II, he defines moral virtue. There, he famously argues that a virtue is "a state of character concerned with choice, lying in a mean, the mean relative to us, this being determined by a rational principle and by that principle by which the man of practical wisdom would determine it" (NE.1106b36–1107a2) We will unpack this definition of moral virtue in Chapter 3. For now, we can point out two of its features that identify it as an instance of the second key concept. First, Aristotle claims that a virtue is a "state of character" – an acquired character trait, rather than a natural faculty. He thinks that we can be praised for our virtues and blamed for our vices, but neither praised nor blamed for natural faculties, since the latter are not sufficiently under our control. Second, Aristotle's definition claims that virtues are "concerned with choice." Specifically, he argues that one cannot have a virtue unless one "choose[s] the [relevant] acts, and choose[s] them for their own sakes" (NE.1105a31–32). In other words, to have the virtue of justice, it is not enough to simply perform just acts – to do what the just person would do. One must perform those acts for the right reasons: because one cares about justice, not because one cares about one's image. Motives matter for virtue.

Does Aristotle think that ends also matter for virtue? To endorse the motives-actions-and-ends variety, he must think that virtue requires getting external goods. Let's briefly look at *Aristotle's* definition of courage. In NE.III, he claims that "the man . . . who faces and who fears the right things and from the right motive, in the right way and at the right time . . . is brave; for the brave man feels and acts according to the merits of the case and in whatever way the rule directs" (NE.111b18–20). Aristotle clearly thinks that a number of things are required for one to have the virtue of courage: the right motives; the right acts – one must face the right things; and the right emotions – one must fear the right things. For now, we will assume that ends and effects are external, and that getting one's acts right is not enough for getting good ends or effects. (We address this issue in Chapter 3.) Does Aristotle think virtue requires producing external goods? On his view, would Alice Paul count as having the virtue of courage if she spoke out about suffrage, feared what she should (violence), and had the right motives (voting equality), but was ineffective due to bad luck? In other words, would she count as having the virtue if, due to bad luck in her political environment (she happened to be in a region controlled by the Taliban), her acts of standing up for suffrage consistently failed to make any actual progress towards suffrage? Philosophers disagree. Some think Aristotle's account of virtue does require the successful production of good effects. Hence, Paul would not count as having the virtue if her acts had consistently backfired. But, others think Aristotle is confused about this point, and that his account of virtue may not require the production of good external effects (Annas 2003). Hence, Paul (as described in this paragraph) would have the virtue of courage, even if her actions had consistently failed to make any actual progress towards suffrage (due to bad luck).

Rosalind Hursthouse is a "neo-Aristotelian." She is a contemporary ethicist who bases her views about the moral virtues on Aristotle's views about the moral virtues. She, too, endorses the second key concept of virtue. Like Aristotle, she thinks that moral virtues and vices are acquired character traits for which we can be praised and blamed. She also explicitly argues that moral virtues require "choice." On her view, "there is more to the possession of a virtue than being disposed to act in certain sorts of ways; at the very least one has to act in those ways for certain sorts of reasons" (1999: 11). To have the virtue of honesty, a person must perform the right acts – she must tell the truth when she should. But, she must also have the right motives – she must tell the truth because she thinks it is right to do so, not because she thinks she would get caught lying. According to Hursthouse, motives matter for virtue. Following Aristotle, she thinks that virtues require getting one's acts, motives, and emotions right. Does she think that they also require getting good ends or effects? In Chapter 3, we will consider whether Hursthouse is a motives-actions-and-ends theorist, or a motives-actions-no-ends theorist. Arguably, she could fall in either camp.

Linda Zagzebski is also a "neo-Aristotelian." She is a contemporary epistemologist who bases her views about the *intellectual* virtues on Aristotle's views about the *moral* virtues. She applies the second key concept to both moral and intellectual virtues. Zagzebski argues that like Aristotle's moral virtues and vices, intellectual virtues and vices are also acquired character traits for which we can be praised and blamed. On her view, the intellectual virtues are character traits like open-mindedness, intellectual courage, and intellectual autonomy; they are not hard-wired capacities like memory and vision. Zagzebski argues that both moral and intellectual virtues require the right motives; performing the right acts is not enough. For instance, to have the intellectual virtue of open-mindedness, one must do more than perform the right intellectual acts – one must do more than consider alternative ideas. One must also have the right intellectual motives – one must care about truth. So, the politician who considers alternative policies, but does so only to get re-elected, is not open-minded. His actions are those that an open-minded person would perform, but his motives are not those of the open-minded person. He is "faking it."

For Zagzebski, motives matter. She and Aristotle agree that virtues require getting one's motives, acts, and emotions right. But, Zagzebski unambiguously argues that virtues require getting good ends or effects. Having the right motives and emotions, and performing the right acts, is not enough for virtue, if one is ineffective. Accordingly, she argues that one won't be open-minded unless one reliably gets true beliefs. If a person is in a deceptive environment, due to bad luck, and gets more false beliefs than true ones, then he isn't open-minded, even if his motives and actions are pristine. In sum,

Zagzebski thinks that a virtue is a "deep and enduring acquired excellence of a person, involving a characteristic motivation to produce a certain desired end and *reliable success* in bringing about that end" (1996: 137; my emphasis.) On her view, reliable success in getting true beliefs matters for intellectual virtue. If a person is massively deceived, she is not intellectually virtuous. Hence, Zagzebski is unambiguously in the motives-actions-and-ends camp.

Like Zagzebski, *James Montmarquet* is a contemporary epistemologist who bases his views about the intellectual virtues on Aristotle's views about the moral virtues. He, too, thinks the intellectual virtues are acquired character traits that require getting one's motives, acts, and emotions right. But, unlike Zagzebski, Montmarquet is unambiguously in the motives-actions-no-ends camp. On his view, getting good ends or effects is not required for intellectual virtue. According to Montmarquet, to have the intellectual virtue of open-mindedness, one must care about getting truths – one must have the right motives. One must also act as the open-minded person would – one must consider alternative ideas when one should. But, one need not actually succeed in getting true beliefs. In his words, "truth-conduciveness cannot . . . be the distinctive mark of the epistemic virtues" (1993: 20). So, if a person consistently cares about truth and consistently considers alternative ideas when she should, she is open-minded. She need not end up with true beliefs. She will be open-minded even if, due to bad luck, she is in a deceptive environment and ends up with more false beliefs than true ones. In short, according to Montmarquet, intellectual virtues require the right motives and the right acts, but do not require getting good ends or effects. One can be massively deceived and still be intellectually virtuous.

Michael Slote is a contemporary ethicist whose views about the moral virtues are largely inspired by David Hume's views rather than Aristotle's. Like Hume, Slote focuses on the virtues of sympathy and empathy.[10] Slote clearly thinks that motives matter for virtue. He argues that to have virtues like benevolence (sympathy) and empathy, one must have the right motives. Specifically, one must strike a balance between caring about friends and family, caring about strangers, and caring about oneself. People who only care about themselves, or about their own friends and families, do not have virtuous motives. Slote thinks that producing good external effects is not required for virtue. Like Montmarquet, Slote is unambiguously in the motives-actions-no-ends camp. In *Morals from Motives*, Slote envisions a person with "fully benevolent or caring motivation" who is, due to no fault of her own, "foiled in her aims," and ends up actually hurting the people she tries to help (2001: 34). He argues that this person "cannot be criticized for acting immorally, however badly things turn out" (2001: 34). In short, Slote thinks getting external goods is not required for virtue. One can produce bad effects and still be morally virtuous. What matters is whether one cares.

1.3 Must We Choose between the Two Key Concepts?

To recap, according to our working definition of virtue, virtues are qualities that make us excellent people. Each of our two key concepts of virtue is compatible with this working definition. The first key concept maintains that virtues require reliable success in getting good ends or effects, but do not require good motives. Here, virtues make us excellent people because having the virtues means that we will consistently get good ends or effects, like well-being and true beliefs. In contrast, the second key concept claims that virtues require good motives, but may or may not require good ends or effects. Here, virtues make us excellent people because having the virtues means that we will consistently care about the well-being of ourselves and others, and about true beliefs. Though these two key concepts are both compatible with our working definition, they are incompatible with each other. If one of them is "the right" concept of virtue, then the other must be wrong. Does this mean that we must choose between them? Does it mean that one of them is "the right" – the real – concept of virtue, and the other is just wrong?

I don't think we need to choose between our two key concepts of virtue. In fact, I think both of them are legitimate, and that neither is any more or less right or real than the other. To see why, let's revisit two of our original examples: House's open-mindedness, and Paul's courage. When we look at patently clear cases of virtue like these, we find that they have some important features in common. For instance, House's open-mindedness and Paul's courage are: (1) acquired character traits that (2) involve performing the right actions. They also (3) consistently produce good ends or effects, like true beliefs and suffrage, and (4) involve good motivations. Recall that neither House nor Paul is motivated by money or fame: House cares about truth, and Paul cares about women getting suffrage. Interestingly, theorists as diverse as Sosa, Zagzebski, and Montmarquet will all *agree* that House has virtue. Sosa will agree because House reliably gets true beliefs. Montmarquet will agree because House has an acquired character trait that involves caring about truth. And Zagzebski will agree for both of these reasons. Likewise, theorists as diverse as Plato, Aristotle, Hursthouse, Driver, and Slote will all *agree* that Paul has virtue. Driver will agree because Paul reliably makes progress toward suffrage – she makes the world a better place for women. Slote will agree because Paul has an acquired character trait that involves good motives – Paul cares about women getting suffrage. Plato, Aristotle, and Hursthouse will (arguably) agree for both of these reasons. What this shows is that when all of (1)–(4) obtain, our philosophers agree about virtue!

They disagree about virtue when some of (1)–(4) are missing. To illustrate: suppose there was a person, call him "House-lite," who was exactly like House, except he didn't reliably get true beliefs – he almost never got the right diagnoses. Here, (3) is clearly missing. Accordingly, Sosa and Zagzebski would claim that House-lite is not virtuous; but Montmarquet would claim that he is. Alternatively, suppose there was a person, call her "Paul-lite," who was exactly like Paul, except she didn't have good motives – she only cared about personal fame. Here, (4) is missing. Consequently, Plato, Aristotle, Hursthouse, and Slote would claim that Paul-lite is not virtuous, but Driver would claim that she is.

What does this show? It shows that disagreements about virtue do not result from a lack of information. All our philosophers agree on the facts – they all agree that House and

Paul satisfy (1)–(4), that House-lite is unreliable, and that Paul-lite has selfish motives. The facts are not in dispute. Instead, their disagreement results from the concept of virtue itself. The concept of virtue – think of our working definition – is vague or thin. It tells us that virtues are excellences, but it does not determine which of conditions (1)–(4) are necessary for something's being an excellence. There are many thin concepts in our language, like our concept of sport. To illustrate: we all agree that football (soccer in the US) is a sport. After all, it is: (i) competitive, (ii) organized, (iii) entertaining, and involves (iv) teamwork and (v) physical skill. But what about golfing, running with a local club, or chess, each of which lacks some of (i)–(v)? Are they sports? Here, we are likely to disagree, depending on which of conditions (i)–(v) each of us favors. The point is that the concept of sport does not determine which of conditions (i)–(v) are necessary. It allows for different combinations. This is what makes the concept of sport thin. As Michael Lynch puts the point, a thin concept is like a roughly drawn sketch that can be completed in different ways (1998: 63). How one completes the sketch will depend on how one "thickens" the concept. Different ways of thickening the concept will result in different pictures, but neither way of thickening the concept is more correct than the other.

The same is true of the concept of virtue (our working definition). The concept of virtue tells us that virtues are excellences, but it does not determine which of conditions (1)–(4) are necessary for something's being an excellence. It allows any combination of (1)–(4) to be necessary. Consequently, Slote's claim that good motives, rather than good effects, are required for virtue is no more correct than Driver's claim that it is good effects, rather than good motives, that are required. Slote has thickened the concept of virtue in one way; Driver has thickened it in a different way. Both of these ways of thickening the concept – both of these uses of "virtue" – are legitimate. There is no single right way to fill in the concept of virtue, just as there is no single right way to fill in a sketch. After all, one way to be an excellent person is to have good motives – to care about the welfare of others, or about truth. Another way to be an excellent person is to reliably get good ends or effects – to make the world better by producing well-being or true beliefs. Since there is no single right way to fill in the concept of virtue, it would be misguided to argue about which of our two key concepts is "the right" or real concept. Both of our key concepts are legitimate ways to thicken our working definition of virtue (Battaly 2001).

1.4   Why Should We Care about the Virtues?

Why are the virtues important? Do virtuous people live better lives than other people? Do they have more knowledge? If they do, these would be good reasons to be virtuous! Several of the philosophers above argue that virtuous people do lead better lives and have more knowledge than the rest of us.

For instance, in one of Plato's dialogues, *Euthydemus*, Socrates argues that being virtuous is sufficient for living a good life (for *eudaimonia*). According to Socrates, all virtuous people live well, simply because they are virtuous. Nothing else is needed to live a good life, not even good luck. We might wonder whether Socrates is correct. Are virtuous people who are ill, unemployed, or friendless living good lives? Are they flourishing?

In contrast with Socrates, Aristotle argues that virtue alone is not enough for living a good life. In addition to virtue, one must also have external goods, like "good birth . . . beauty," wealth, and friends (NE.1099b2–3). One disadvantage of Aristotle's view is that it is difficult to determine exactly which external goods are required for living a good life. Aristotle seems to recognize that the rich and beautiful have easier lives than the rest of us. But, can't we have good lives too? Similarly, if health is required for living well, does this mean that persons with disabilities cannot live well? Do we really want to claim that being rich, beautiful, and healthy are required for living well? One advantage of Aristotle's view is that it recognizes that living well is not entirely up to us. Suppose that some degree of health, wealth, and freedom are required for living well. These are goods over which we have little control. Had I been born 100 years earlier in the US, I would not have had the right to vote. When and where one is born, the family one is born into, and the economic resources of that family are all matters of luck. If Aristotle is right, and living well does require external goods, then this gives us reason to help improve living conditions around the world, so that more people can reach the thresholds of health and wealth that are needed for flourishing.

Though Aristotle thinks that virtue is not sufficient for living well, he does think it is necessary. This means that rich, beautiful, and popular people won't live well unless they are also just, courageous, temperate, and wise. Is Aristotle correct? Or, do badly behaved celebrities live well? The above arguments about virtue and living well are addressed in Chapter 6.

What about knowledge? Do virtuous people have more knowledge? Both Sosa and Zagzebski think that we need the intellectual virtues (or components of them) in order to get knowledge. For instance, Sosa thinks that we can't have visual knowledge without the virtue of reliable vision. Accordingly, Mr. Magoo, the extremely near-sighted protagonist of the 1960s cartoon series by the same name, lacks visual knowledge. Magoo's vision is famously unreliable – it produces many more false beliefs about his surroundings than true ones. Sosa's point is that even in cases where Magoo's vision happens to produce true beliefs about his surroundings, he doesn't have knowledge. Magoo lacks knowledge because he only ends up with true beliefs due to good luck; and lucky guesses are not knowledge. Zagzebski thinks that knowledge requires us: to have the same motivations as the intellectually virtuous person; to perform the acts that an intellectually virtuous person would perform; and to get true beliefs as a result. To illustrate: we can't know that, say, the butler committed the crime unless we have intellectually virtuous motivations – we care about getting the truth; we do what an intellectually virtuous person would do in this situation – we gather evidence and consider alternative suspects; and we arrive at a true belief as a result of these actions and motivations. Are Sosa and Zagzebski correct? One potential problem with Zagzebski's view is that it might

2
Ends Matter: Virtues Attain Good Ends or Effects

The working definition of virtue in Chapter 1 tells us that virtues are qualities that make one an excellent person. There, we identified two key ways to be an excellent person: by getting good ends or effects, or having good motives. This chapter focuses on the first key concept of virtue: what makes a quality a virtue is its success in getting good ends or effects. Good motives are not required. According to this concept, it is good ends or effects – like well-being, health, knowledge, and truth – that ultimately matter; they are intrinsically valuable. Virtues matter because they attain those good ends or effects. In short, a quality is a virtue if and only if it reliably "gets the goods."

The first key concept entails two conditions. First, a quality is a virtue only if it reliably gets the goods: if a quality does not reliably get the goods, then it is not a virtue. In other words, getting the goods is *necessary* for virtue. It doesn't matter how hard one tries, or how good one's motives are; if one fails to reliably deliver the goods, one doesn't have virtues. To illustrate, consider Doug Murphy, a medical intern on the television comedy *Scrubs* (NBC, 2001–10). Doug has good motives – he cares about his patients and tries to make them well. But, despite his best efforts, he routinely kills them! Since Doug fails to reliably deliver the good of health, he fails to have the virtues associated with the practice of medicine. Analogously, consider the caring but failing student, who genuinely wants to learn (say) logic, but can't seem to figure it out. She studies hard, and actually cares about the material, but still fails her exams. Since this student fails to deliver the goods – here, truths in logic – she fails to have the intellectual virtues associated with that subject. In short, according to the first key concept, reliable success in getting good ends or effects is required for virtue.

Second, reliable success in getting the goods is also *sufficient* for virtue. That is, if a quality reliably gets the goods, it is a virtue. This is so even if it involves inferior motives. Recall, for instance, the character Russell in the animated film *Up* (Pixar, 2009). Russell is a "Wilderness Explorer" who helps the isolated widower and protagonist of the film, Carl Fredericksen. Russell clearly succeeds in helping Fredericksen: he helps him fulfill his dream of traveling to Paradise Falls, and, more importantly, opens the grieving Fredericksen up to new friendships. But, Russell does not help Fredericksen because he cares about Fredericksen for his own sake; instead, his motives are selfish – he wants to earn his "Assisting the Elderly Badge" and become a "Senior Wilderness Explorer." (Even if Russell's motives are not bad for a child,[1] they are still less than ideal – it would be better if Russell were motivated to help Fredericksen because he cared about *him*.) Now, imagine that Russell grows up to be an adult who consistently succeeds in helping others, but does so for selfish reasons. According to the first key concept, he would still have the virtue of benevolence, since he reliably succeeds in bringing about the well-being of others – he gets the goods. Alternatively, consider James Watson and Francis Crick, who were the first to discover the double-helix structure of DNA. Watson and Crick were motivated to get truths about DNA, and cared about understanding its structure. But arguably, their primary motives were winning the Nobel Prize, and having their names attached to DNA in perpetuity.[2] Watson and Crick clearly delivered the goods on this occasion – they discovered important truths about DNA. Let's assume that they were also *reliably* successful at producing truths in their areas of expertise. Consequently, the first key concept claims that they have intellectual virtues, despite their narcissistic motives for fame.

According to the first key concept, any quality that reliably attains good ends or effects counts as a virtue. Hence, virtues will be a diverse lot. Some will be moral; and others intellectual. Some will be natural capacities; some acquired skills; and some acquired character traits. Virtues are not even exclusive to people in general. Skilled professionals (doctors), animals (racehorses), and objects (knives) can have virtues. Still, our focus will be on qualities that make us excellent as people in general, since this is something we all have in common, irrespective of our differing jobs and roles.

Despite their diversity, all of these virtues are reliable. Virtues are qualities that *reliably* succeed in producing good ends or effects. What does this mean? To say that a virtue reliably produces good ends or effects is to say that it produces more good ends or effects than bad ones. How many more? For starters, the percentage must be above 50, but it can fall short of 100. To reliably produce good effects, one must produce good effects more often than not. But, reliability can fall short of perfection – even virtuous people occasionally fail to get good ends. There is a wide continuum remaining. Must the percentage of good ends be more than 60, or 75, or 90? This is tricky, and depends on whether we think virtues must meet a minimum threshold, or whether they must approach perfection. There are benefits to leaving the percentage unspecified, though it may seem like a cop-out. The benefit is that doing so will allow us to consider the threshold view, the near-perfection view, and everything in between. We don't want to rule any of these out at the start.

2.1   Virtues Attain Good Ends: The Teleological Variety

There are two varieties of the first key concept of virtue: the teleological and the nonteleological varieties. The teleological variety argues that virtues reliably succeed in attaining good *ends*. Introduced in Chapter 1, teleology is the view that things and people have built-in ends or functions. Plato and Aristotle are two of its most famous proponents. They argue that things, animals, "craftsmen," classes of people, and people in general all have built-in ends or functions. For instance, they think the function (end) of an ear is to hear, of a knife is to cut, of a racehorse is to run, of a guardian is to rule (see below), and of a person-in-general is (roughly) to engage in rational activity. Some of these functions are allegedly built in by nature – like the functions of an ear, a guardian (for Plato), and a person-in-general; while others are built-into artifacts or animals by us – we design knives to cut.

The teleological variety of our first key concept makes two important claims:

(TI)   It defines virtues and vices in terms of built-in functions or ends.
(TII) It uses these functions (ends) to explain why virtues are valuable and vices are not.

Let's begin with (TI). According to (TI), virtues just are qualities that enable a person or thing to perform its function well – to attain its end. Likewise, vices just are qualities that explain why a person or thing is performing its function poorly – failing to attain its end. This means that *anything* with a function (end) will have virtues and vices: ears, knives, racehorses, and people in general will each have their own respective sets of virtues and vices. So, the teleological variety claims that *for any X with a function (end), the virtues of X are the qualities that enable X to perform its function well (to attain its end)*; and the vices of X are the qualities that explain why X is performing its function poorly (failing to attain its end).

How do we identify the virtues and vices of a knife, an ear, and, most importantly, a person-in-general? In each case, we do so by *first* identifying the end (function) of the X in question. We *then* determine which qualities enable (virtues) or prevent (vices) the X in question from getting its end. To illustrate, suppose we were to agree that the end (function) of a knife is to cut. We could then identify some of the virtues of a knife, like heft and sharpness, which are qualities that enable knives to cut well. Following the same pattern, we would identify the virtues of a person-in-general by first locating the end of a person-in-general. For the moment, imagine we were to agree that the end of a person-in-general is rational activity (as Aristotle claims). We might then argue that the virtues of a person-in-general include open-mindedness and courage, provided that open-mindedness and courage enable us to excel at rational activity.

Let's move on to (TII). Virtues are valuable; vices are not. Where does the value of the virtues come from? In other words, what makes the virtues of a knife valuable? And, more importantly, what makes the virtues of a person-in-general valuable? (TII) argues that virtues derive their value from the value of the end (function) in question. So, the virtues of a knife are valuable because the end (function) of a knife – cutting – is valuable. Likewise, the virtues of a person-in-general are valuable because the end (function) of a person-in-general – whatever that turns out to be – is valuable. In short, virtues are valuable because they get good ends.

According to the teleological variety, ends are what ultimately matter; and some of these ends matter more than others. Some ends, like the end of a person-in-general, are said to be intrinsically valuable – valuable for their own sakes. Other ends, like cutting, are said to be instrumentally or constitutively valuable. On the teleological view, the virtues themselves are rarely thought to be intrinsically valuable; rather they are thought to be valuable because they *get* good ends. Hence, the virtues are instrumentally or constitutively valuable (or both), since they are means to, or parts of, good ends.

2.1.1 The Function and Virtues of a Person: Plato and Aristotle

The most famous endorsements of the teleological variety occur in Plato's *Republic* and Aristotle's *Nicomachean Ethics*. Plato and Aristotle both use the functions of body parts, artifacts, animals, and "craftsmen" to argue that people-in-general have a function. They then use the function of a person-in-general to identify the virtues of a person-in-general. Let's begin by explaining their arguments.

Plato: Republic

In his conversation with Thrasymachus at *Republic* 353, Socrates (speaking for Plato) argues that ears, eyes, knives, and horses each have specific functions. The specific or "proper" function of a thing is "what it alone can do or what it does better than anything else" (353a). For instance, the specific function of a pruning knife is pruning, of a carving knife is carving, and so on. At *Republic* 353d–e, Plato argues that a person – a "soul" – also has a specific function, which includes *ruling* oneself, *deliberating*, and *living*. In his words: "Is there some function of a soul that you couldn't perform with anything else, for example, taking care of things, ruling, deliberating, and the like? Is there anything other than a soul to which you could rightly assign these, and say that they are its peculiar function? . . . What of living? Isn't that a function of the soul?"

Plato assumes that the above passage shows that a person-in-general has a function. He also assumes that he has identified what that function is. In the same passage, he defines the virtues teleologically: "anything that has a function performs it well by means of its own peculiar virtue and badly by means of its vice" (353c). Accordingly, he sets out to find the virtues of a person – the qualities that enable us to function well: to rule ourselves well, deliberate well, and live well. In *Republic*, he does this by first identifying the virtues of the *polis* (state), which he thinks are analogous to the virtues of an individual person, but "larger" and easier to spot (368d–e).

Plato argues that the function of the state is to meet the needs of its citizens – to provide food, clothing, housing, health, entertainment, and defense. There are three classes of people in Plato's *polis*, each with its own function. The class of "craftsmen" – which includes farmers, builders, doctors, and musicians – has the function of providing food, health, and durable goods. The class of auxiliaries (soldiers) has the function of defending the state. The class of guardians, the highest class, has the function of ruling the state. Plato contends that each person is naturally suited to perform only one of these functions (*Republic* 370b). Some people are naturally suited to be craftsmen of a particular type, others to defend the state as auxiliaries, and the special few to rule as guardians. The sorting hat in the *Harry Potter* series is similarly Platonic – dividing students into houses in accordance with their natural aptitudes.

Plato also thinks that each person should perform the function – do the job – for which she is naturally suited. If people did jobs for which they were not naturally suited, then the state would end in "ruin" (*Republic* 434b). To put the same point differently, class mobility is forbidden in Plato's *polis*. Plato simultaneously argues that each person should *only* do the work for which she is naturally suited, since it is "impossible for a single person to practice many . . . professions well" (*Republic* 374a). So, no one works two jobs in Plato's *polis* either.

On Plato's view, all of this ensures that the *polis* is functioning well – that it is "completely good" (*Republic* 427e) – and, thus, that it has the virtues: qualities that enable it to function well. Those virtues are: wisdom, courage, temperance, and justice. The *polis* is wise because its guardians know what is good for the state as a whole. Wisdom enables the guardians to rule the state well. The *polis* is courageous because its auxiliaries fear only what they should. Courage enables the auxiliaries to defend the state well. The *polis* is temperate because its craftsmen submit to the rule of the guardians, allowing the guardians to regulate their inferior desires. Temperance enables the craftsmen to do their jobs, preventing them from running amok. Finally, the *polis* is just because each of the three classes does the work for which it is naturally suited, without meddling in the work of the other classes. Justice is the virtue that enables all of the classes in the *polis* to function well as a coherent whole, without conflict.

Plato thinks that the virtues of individual people are analogous in structure to the virtues of the *polis*. Accordingly, he argues that each person has a tripartite soul, composed of reason, spirit, and appetite. Each part of the soul has its own function. The function of reason (like that of the guardians) is to know what is good for oneself as a whole, and ultimately to rule the soul. Knowing what is good for oneself as a whole includes knowing which desires are important and knowing which things should be feared. For example, is it more important to satisfy my desire for copious amounts of gin or my desire to finish the paper due tomorrow? Reason can function well or poorly. Plato argues that the virtue of wisdom enables reason to function well, since the wise person succeeds in *knowing* what is good for the "whole soul" (*Republic* 442c). In other words, the wise person's beliefs about what should be desired and what should be feared are true. The wise person makes good judgments about what is best overall – she knows that the desire to finish the paper is more important. In contrast, those who lack wisdom make bad judgments about what is best overall – they falsely believe that the desire for gin is more important. Recall that, for Plato, *deliberating* – making judgments about what is best overall – is one of the functions of a person-in-general. Wisdom is the virtue that enables us to perform this function well.

The function of spirit (like that of the auxiliaries) is to enforce reason's decisions about what is good for the person as a whole. Specifically, its goal is to preserve "through pains and pleasures the declarations of reason about what is to be feared and what isn't" (*Republic* 442c). For instance, reason might tell us that we should not be afraid of surgery despite the pain that it will cause; or that we should fear addiction to drugs despite the pleasure they produce. The job of spirit is to enforce the dictates of reason. Spirit can function well or poorly. Plato thinks that the virtue of courage enables spirit to function well, since the courageous person fears all and only what he should. In contrast, those who lack courage are persuaded by pleasure or pain to ignore some of the dictates of reason. They fear what they shouldn't (surgery) or fail to fear what they should (drug addiction).

The function of appetite (like that of the craftsmen) is to obey reason's decisions about what should and should not be desired. Appetite can also function well or poorly. Plato argues that the virtue of temperance enables appetite to function well, since the temperate person desires only what she should. In contrast, those who lack temperance desire what they shouldn't – they ignore some of the dictates of reason. They desire the gin!

Finally, justice is the virtue that enables each part of the soul to do its own work, in concert with the other parts. In

Plato's words, the just person "does not allow any part of himself to do the work of another part or allow the various classes within himself to meddle with each other" (*Republic* 443d). Justice enables the person to function well as a coherent whole, without internal conflict. Recall that for Plato, *ruling* oneself and *living* are the two remaining functions of a person-in-general. Arguably, the four virtues working together enable us to perform these functions well.

Aristotle: Nicomachean Ethics *I*

Aristotle also argues that a person-in-general has a function, and uses that function to identify our virtues. His main argument for the function of a person occurs in *Nicomachean Ethics* I, the primary goal of which is to define human flourishing (*eudaimonia*) or living well. Accordingly, the function of a person does double duty for Aristotle: he uses it to identify human virtues *and* to identify the good life (*eudaimonia*).

In NE.I.7, Aristotle argues that "craftsmen" have specific functions. The function of a flute-player is to play the flute; of a sculptor is to sculpt, and so on. Likewise, each body part – eyes, hands, feet – has its own function. Aristotle infers that since craftsmen and body parts have functions, people-in-general also have a function – it would be odd if craftsmen and body parts had functions but people-in-general didn't. What is the function of a person-in-general? Aristotle considers three alternatives. First, he argues that our function cannot be growth, since it must be something that is distinctively human. Nor can our function be perception, since we share perception with animals. Having ruled out growth and perception, Aristotle endorses the third and final option he considers: "an active life of the element that has a rational principle"; that is, *rational activity* (NE.1098a4). Rational activity is, roughly, activity that involves reason. This, he thinks, is distinctively human.

Is *rational activity* limited to thinking? Not for Aristotle. He argues that there are two kinds of rational activity, each of which corresponds to a different part of the soul: a rational part and an appetitive (desiring) part. For Aristotle, rational activity includes thinking – contemplating theories and calculating what to do – which is the hallmark of the rational part of the soul. But, rational activity also includes following the dictates of reason: wanting, fearing, and doing what reason tells us. This applies to the appetitive (desiring) part of the soul. So, part of our function is to think, and part of our function is to follow reason (we can do each well or poorly). In sum, Aristotle thinks the function of a person is "an activity of soul which follows *or* implies a rational principle" (NE.1098a7–8; my emphasis). The function of the appetitive part is to follow reason; the function of the rational part is to imply reason.

Which qualities enable us to perform these functions well – to excel at *rational activity*? Aristotle argues that since there are two different kinds of rational activity, there are also two different kinds of virtue – intellectual and moral. The virtues of the rational part are intellectual. They enable us to get theoretical and practical truths – to excel at thinking (see below). The virtues of the appetitive part are moral. They enable us to desire, fear, and do what reason tells us – to excel at following reason. Aristotle's list of moral virtues is extensive. It includes courage, temperance, justice, and even pride and wit. To briefly introduce one of these virtues, courage is a disposition to fear and yet face "the right things and from the right motive, in the right way and at the right time" (NE.1115b18–19). Which things, motives, ways, and times are "right"? This is determined by the intellectual virtue of practical wisdom, which plays a role in all the moral virtues. Accordingly, the courageous person fears and acts the way reason says she should.[3]

How does Aristotle use the function of a person to identify *eudaimonia*, or living well? In a famous passage in NE.I.7, he uses (a) the function of a person, along with (b) the teleological notion of virtue and (c) a teleological notion of the good, to generate a definition of living well. He begins by advocating a *teleological notion of the good*: "for a flute-player, a sculptor . . . and, in general, for all things that have a function or activity, the good and 'the well' is thought to reside in the function" (NE.1097b26–7). Roughly, *for any X with a function (end), X is good if and only if X performs its function well (attains its end)*. So, just as a flute player is good if and only if he plays the flute well, and an eye is good if and only if it sees well, a person will be good if and only if he performs *his* specific function – rational activity – well. What enables a person or thing to perform its function well? Virtues, of course! Aristotle endorses the teleological notion of virtue: for any X with a function (end), the virtues of X are the qualities that enable X to perform its function well (to attain its end). Combining these elements, he infers that a person will be good if and only if he engages in virtuous rational activity. He concludes that human flourishing – living well – has virtuous rational activity at its core. To flourish – to live well – we must lead active lives of virtue.[4]

Objections

The teleological variety of our first key concept claims that a person cannot have virtues without a function. Recall (TI) above. But, have Plato and Aristotle successfully shown that people have a function? And, if so, have they correctly identified that function? Finally, regarding (TII), have they successfully accounted for the value of our virtues?

First, Plato and Aristotle argue that a person has a specific function because body parts, artifacts, animals, classes of people, and craftsmen each have their own specific functions. But, we might worry that their arguments commit us to a controversial claim: that people are assigned a function, or designed to perform it, by someone or something else. This is controversial because in philosophy we don't get designers for free – we have to argue for the existence of God or gods. Why would the arguments above commit us to the existence of a designer, or at least an "assigner"? Because *we* assign functions to artifacts, craftsmen, classes of people, and even animals. We need to cut things; so we assign a function to knives and design them accordingly. We value music, health, defense, and leadership; so we write job descriptions for flute players, doctors, soldiers, and "rulers." Moreover, we might think that these things (artifacts, craftsmen, classes of people, and animals) have functions *only* insofar as we assign or design them. In other words, if we didn't assign these things functions, they wouldn't have functions at all. So, contra Plato, the functions of a guardian and a sculptor are *not* built in by nature; instead, they are assigned by us.

In short, the worry is that arguments for the function of a person ask us to draw the same conclusion about people – we have a function because someone or something else assigned it to us or designed us to perform it. This is where some of us will balk.

Second, the objection above does not apply as easily to body parts, since we did not design them. But, we do use body parts as tools to serve our interests. We use ears to hear, eyes to see, feet to stand, etc. Now, suppose that body parts have functions *only* insofar as we use them: if we didn't use them to serve our interests, they wouldn't have functions at all. It would then follow that for a person to have a function, someone or something must use people as tools. This, too, is controversial. We don't get "users" for free either.

What happens if the functions of body parts do *not* depend solely on our interests and use – if body parts *do* have functions that are built in by nature? Would it then follow that people have our own function that is built in by nature? More broadly, if the parts of a thing have functions, does the whole thing also have its own special function? This line of reasoning is more promising. It is promising because there are lots of examples in which things that have functional parts also have their own functions. Take bicycles. Bicycles have functional parts precisely because they have a function as a whole; and their function as a whole is distinct from the mere sum of the functions of each of their parts. The same is meant to be true of us – our function as a whole (e.g., rational activity) is supposed to be distinct from the mere sum of the functions of our body parts (e.g., seeing + hearing, etc.) So far, so good. But, the success of this line of reasoning is uncertain, because its clearest instances are all things designed by us. To avoid begging the question against the first objection, we need to consider something that isn't designed by us. To that end, let's suppose that tigers have body parts (feet, etc.) whose functions are built in by nature. Do tigers thereby have special functions of their own? The answer isn't obvious. On the one hand, we might argue that they do have special functions in relation to the broader ecosystem; or that the special function of a tiger is to be a good specimen of its kind. But, on the other hand, we might contend that tigers do not have any special functions or purposes of their own; and that for a tiger, the function of being a good specimen of its kind is nothing over and above the sum of the functions of each of its body parts. In short, the jury is still out.

Third, let's be charitable and assume, for the moment, that functions of parts and wholes can be built in by nature. We might still object to Plato's and Aristotle's assumption that eyes, feet, etc. each have a *single* natural function. Why don't they each have multiple functions? Arguably, eyes don't just have the function of seeing, they also have the function of crying. Likewise, feet have the functions of standing *and* walking; etc. The same can be said of people: we are, as it were, multitaskers, with multiple functions that are specific to us.

Fourth, have Plato and Aristotle correctly identified the functions specific to us? If not, they will not correctly identify our virtues. Plato argues that our function includes deliberating, ruling, and living; Aristotle thinks it consists in rational activity. Aristotle only considers two other options (nutrition and perception), ruling them out on the grounds that we share them with other species. But, what about imagination, comedy, lying, or weakness of will, all of which seem to be distinctive of us as a species? Shouldn't these be considered in addition to deliberation and rational activity? Are deliberation and ruling even unique to our species?

Finally, what about (TII)? Even if Plato and Aristotle could answer all the above objections, we might still argue that they haven't successfully accounted for the *value* of our virtues. Recall that according to the teleological variety of our first key concept, virtues get their value from the value of the end (function) in question. Ends are what ultimately matter. Virtues are valuable because they are means to, or parts of, good ends. Let's assume, for the moment, that Plato and Aristotle succeed in identifying the end of a person. What is the *value* of that end (function) – in what way is it good? Plato and Aristotle use a *teleological notion of the good* to link functioning well (attaining the end) with being good. They think that for any X with a function (end), X is good if and only if X performs its function well (attains its end). Accordingly, a flute player is good if and only if he plays the flute well, the *polis* is good if and only if it provides for its citizens well, and a person is good if and only if she reasons well.

So, what is the problem? According to the teleological notion of the good, *anything* with a function can be good, even liars and racists. So, in the same way that James Galway is a good flute player, Bernie Madoff is a good liar and Strom Thurmond is a good racist. After all, Madoff and Thurmond performed the functions of a liar and a racist well. Madoff defrauded thousands of people, and Thurmond espoused racism in the US Senate for decades. If you doubt that good liars and racists are sanctioned kinds, consider good soldiers and executioners, who are efficient at killing. What these examples show is that one can be good in the teleological sense without being objectively good. The teleological notion of the good only tells us when something or someone is a *good specimen of its kind*. It does not tell us whether it is objectively good to be a good specimen of that kind. To tell us that, the teleological notion of the good would have to evaluate the end of X as objectively good or bad. But this is exactly what it fails to do! To put the same point differently, the teleological notion of the good allows the end of X to be objectively bad. Similarly, the teleological notion of virtue only tells us when something or someone has qualities that enable it to attain its end. It does not tell us whether the end, or the qualities, in question are objectively good or bad. To put the same point differently, the teleological notion of virtue allows objectively bad qualities to count as "virtues." It counts dishonesty, dogmatism, and callousness as "virtues" of liars, racists, and soldiers because these qualities enable them to attain their ends.[5]

Something has gone very wrong. The problem is that the very same teleological notions are supposed to explain why the virtues of a person are valuable – why they are objectively good. But, teleological notions won't explain that. To explain what makes the virtues of a person objectively good, we need an additional argument that the end of a person is objectively good. Of course, Plato and Aristotle do provide additional arguments, though we won't address them here. The point is just that we need additional arguments; teleological notions are not enough.

2.1.2 *Intellectual Ends and Virtues: Aristotle and Sosa*

Aristotle: Nicomachean Ethics *VI*

Aristotle argues that people can have two different kinds of virtues: moral and intellectual. In NE.I.13, he contends that moral virtues attain the end of the appetitive (desiring) part of the soul; whereas intellectual virtues attain the end of the rational part of the soul. Moral virtues like courage and temperance enable us to obey the truths generated by the rational part of the soul; whereas, intellectual virtues like practical wisdom enable us to generate those truths in the first place.

What exactly is the end of the rational part of the soul? In NE.VI, Aristotle argues that the rational part of the soul is itself subdivided into two parts – a theoretical or "contemplative" part, and a practical or "calculative" part – each with its own end. He defines the ends of the two parts as follows: "of the intellect which is contemplative, not practical nor productive, the good and the bad state are truth and falsity respectively (for this is the work of everything intellectual); while of the part which is practical and intellectual the good state is truth in agreement with right desire" (NE.1139a26–31). In other words, the end of the contemplative part is: truth about theoretical matters. Its function is to generate "invariable" necessary truths, like truths in math and geometry. In contrast, the end of the calculative part is: truth about practical matters in combination with appropriate desires. Its function is to generate "variable" contingent truths, like truths about how to act, and how to make things; for example, given my current circumstances, I should finish tomorrow's presentation rather than drink lots of gin.[6] On Aristotle's view, the end of the calculative part includes appropriate desires because we can't calculate how to act appropriately when our desires are vicious: vicious desires pollute the way we see the world and distort which actions we recognize as options open to us. In contrast, the contemplative part is neither "practical nor productive" – it "moves nothing"; in other words, it is devoid of desire and action (NE.1139a36).

Having established the ends of the contemplative and calculative parts, Aristotle sets out to identify the virtues of each part. He endorses (TI) above: "The work [end] of both the intellectual parts . . . is truth. Therefore, the states that are most strictly those in respect of which each of these parts will reach truth are the virtues of the two parts" (NE.1139b12–14). He identifies three virtues of the contemplative part – scientific knowledge (*episteme),* intuitive reason (*nous*), and philosophical wisdom (*sophia*) – and two primary virtues of the calculative part – skill (*techne*) and practical wisdom (*phronesis*).

On Aristotle's view, *episteme* is the ability to deduce "invariable," or necessary, truths from premises that are necessarily true and self-evident (NE.VI.3). For instance, we employ *episteme* when we deduce theorems in math or geometry from definitions and axioms. We can think of *episteme* as a special, infallible kind of deduction – it is guaranteed to produce true beliefs. (Deduction includes, but is broader than, *episteme*; deduction can involve contingent claims, some of which are false.) *Nous* is what enables us to know the premises in those deductions (NE.VI.6). In other words, *nous* gets us knowledge of self-evident "first principles," like definitions and axioms, for which "no reason can be given" (NE.1142a26). We can think of *nous* as being roughly equivalent to intuitive reason, or a priori insight – it is the ability to immediately know necessary truths. *Sophia* combines *episteme* and *nous.* In Aristotle's words, "the wise man must not only know what follows from the first principles, but must also possess truth about the first principles. Therefore wisdom must be intuitive reason combined with scientific knowledge" (NE.1141a17–19). In other words, it is possible to have the ability to know first principles, without having the ability to deduce anything from them. Likewise, it is possible to have the ability to mechanically deduce theorems without having the ability to know first principles. *Sophia* is the ability to do both: deduce theorems and know first principles. *Nous, episteme*, and *sophia* all produce necessary truths. This is what makes them contemplative virtues – they attain the end of the contemplative part. *Nous* produces the first principles, *episteme* deduces theorems, and *sophia* does both. All three are infallible (Battaly 2014a).

The two primary virtues of the calculative part are *techne* and *phronesis*. Aristotle argues that both of these virtues produce contingent truths: the former about how to make things, the latter about how to act. Roughly, *techne* (skill) is the ability to make things as a result of knowing how to do so. In Aristotle's words, *techne* is a "capacity to make" that involves "a true course of reasoning," whereas lack of *techne* is "concerned with making" but involves a "false course of reasoning" or no reasoning at all (NE.1140a20–22). Skilled architects, doctors, and tennis players all have *techne*. Take, for instance, Rafael Nadal. Nadal has successfully hit thousands of forehands, and has done so because he *knows* how to hit forehands – he knows how to angle his racquet, shift his weight, follow through, etc. He has thought it through. In contrast, consider the tennis novice who lacks *techne*. The novice may occasionally succeed in hitting forehands, but when he does, it is due to "beginner's luck" – unlike Nadal, the novice does not yet *know* what he is doing. In short, *techne* produces truths about how to "make" something – a building, a healthy patient, or a shot in tennis. On Aristotle's view, *techne* also requires having desires – for example, wanting to hit a forehand. This is because *techne* requires a degree of success in, for example, hitting forehands; and merely knowing how to hit a forehand isn't enough to get us to do it. We must also want to do it. Hence, *techne* attains the end of the calculative part – it produces contingent truths and requires corresponding desires. This is what makes it a calculative virtue.

Phronesis (practical wisdom) is the most complicated virtue of any that Aristotle lists. Very roughly, it is the ability to act rightly as a result of knowing what ought to be done. According to Aristotle, *phronesis* is a "true and reasoned . . . capacity to act with regard to the things that are good or bad for man" (NE.1140b4–5) In other words, the person with *phronesis* knows which actions are conducive to the good life. She deliberates well, judges well, and perceives the world as she should. She *recognizes* opportunities for courage, benevolence, temperance, and justice. She also *knows*, for example, when and what she should face and when and from what she should flee; and when and whom she should help and when and whom she shouldn't. So, *phronesis* produces truths about which actions should be performed. It is what enables a morally virtuous person to determine the mean in her actions. But, *phronesis* also requires having morally virtuous desires; this for two reasons. First, *phronesis* requires that one act well, and acting well requires wanting to do what should be done; knowing what should be done is insufficient for action. Second, Aristotle argues that if we do not have morally virtuous desires, then we will overlook opportunities for courage, benevolence, temperance, and justice. We will see the world incorrectly, through the prism of inferior motives. So, on Aristotle's view, not only is *phronesis* needed for moral virtue (without *phronesis* we can't figure out the mean), moral virtue is needed for *phronesis* (without moral virtue we would size up the world incorrectly). For now, the main point is that *phronesis* attains the end of the calculative part – it produces contingent truths and requires appropriate desires. This is what makes it a calculative virtue. Unlike the contemplative virtues, *techne* and *phronesis* are fallible.

Ernest Sosa

Ernest Sosa, a contemporary epistemologist, employs both varieties of the first key concept of virtue. When endorsing the teleological variety, he follows Aristotle both in identifying truth as our chief *intellectual* end, and in arguing that the qualities that enable us to attain that end are intellectual virtues. Accordingly, Sosa claims that "grasping the truth about one's environment" is one of the "proper ends of human beings." And, that "there is a . . . sense of 'virtue' . . . in which anything with a function – natural or artificial – does have virtues. The eye does, after all, have its virtues, and so does a knife" (1991: 271).[7]

Though Sosa and Aristotle agree that getting truths is our chief intellectual function, they focus on different kinds of truths. Aristotle is primarily interested in distinguishing necessary truths (and the qualities that get them) from contingent truths about how to act or make things (and the qualities that get *them*). Hence, his further subdivision of the rational part of the soul into a contemplative part and a calculative part. In contrast, Sosa is primarily interested in contingent truths about our surroundings (and the qualities that get *those* truths). To illustrate, Sosa focuses on truths like "The car is red," "My class starts at 10 a.m.," and "In 2012, Obama was elected President of the US." Such truths are not necessary – though they are actually true, they could have been false. Nor are they practical in Aristotle's sense – they are not truths about how to act or make things. Rather, they are contingent *and* theoretical. Though these truths cut across the two categories Aristotle addresses (theoretical necessary truths; and contingent practical truths), they are *undeniably* the stars of contemporary epistemology.[8]

Sosa and Aristotle also agree that the intellectual virtues are qualities that enable us to get truths. But, since they are interested in getting different kinds of truths, they identify different intellectual virtues. Aristotle's contemplative virtues, which get us necessary truths, are infallible and theoretical (they do not require desire or action); whereas his calculative virtues, which get us truths about how to act and make things, are fallible and practical (they do require desire and action). In contrast, Sosa identifies virtues like vision, memory, deduction, and induction, which get us contingent truths about our surroundings. These virtues are fallible *and* theoretical (they do not require desire or action).

Sosa's main view is that the intellectual virtues are reliable belief-forming faculties or skills, the paradigms of which include reliable vision, memory, induction, and deduction. There are three important features of Sosa's view. First and foremost, the intellectual virtues are reliable – they get us more truths than falsehoods, and thus attain our chief intellectual end. Accordingly, Hermione's memory counts as an intellectual virtue because it is reliable – it produces *more* true beliefs than false ones. Of course, even Hermione isn't perfect. But, on Sosa's view, intellectual virtues need only produce a preponderance of true beliefs – they need not be infallible. Likewise, qualities that produce a preponderance of false beliefs are intellectual vices. The memory of a person suffering from Alzheimer's is a vice because it produces more false beliefs than true ones. Sosa points out that the reliability of a cognitive faculty or skill does not require that it produce truths in highly unusual conditions. "What is required is only that your attempts tend to succeed when circumstances are normal" (2007: 84). For instance, the reliability of the faculty of vision is not impugned by its failure to issue true beliefs about objects that are in the dark. Nor is it impugned by its failure to issue true beliefs about an object's very complex shape (e.g., chiliagon) or specific color (e.g., sand dune). But, it *is* impugned by its failure to issue true beliefs about basic shape and color in conditions that we ordinarily encounter. In other words, its reliability is indexed to conditions (C) in which one sees objects in good lighting, and to fields of propositions (F) that are about the object's basic shape, color, and so on. Accordingly, Sosa argues that to be reliable, and hence a virtue, one's vision must be disposed to produce a preponderance of true beliefs about the basic colors and shapes of medium-sized objects (F), when one sees those objects nearby, without obstruction, and in good lighting (C).[9]

Second, Sosa argues that intellectual virtues can be hard-wired or acquired. In his words, "much of our intellectual competence comes with our brains, but much is due to learning" (2007: 86). Vision, if reliable, is a hard-wired virtue: our brains are wired to produce beliefs based on visual experience. In contrast, interpreting MRI films would be an acquired virtue. It takes time and practice to reliably produce true beliefs about a patient's condition based on MRI films. Perhaps, something similar can be said of deduction. Basic deduction, if reliable, may also be a hard-wired virtue: our brains may be wired to automatically perform some very simple deductions. For instance, when we come to believe that "William and Kate are at the palace," our brains may automatically produce the further belief that "William is at the palace." In contrast, doing derivations in logic would be an acquired virtue. Even if basic deduction is hard-wired, it takes concerted practice and effort to learn how to reliably deduce conclusions from premises by using derivations.

Third, Sosa thinks that intellectual virtues do not require desire or action. (In this respect, they are like Aristotelian contemplative virtues.) Hard-wired virtues like vision do not require any learned desire to care appropriately about the truth. Nor do such hard-wired virtues require intellectual actions. Intellectual actions are (roughly) acts that an agent intentionally performs in acquiring beliefs; for example, considering objections, looking for evidence, constructing arguments, testing hypotheses, etc. As long as our brains (and eyes) are functioning well, hard-wired virtues like vision will reliably produce true beliefs without our intentionally doing anything.[10]

Objections

Echoing the fourth objection at the end of section 2.1.1 (see page 43), have Aristotle and Sosa correctly identified our intellectual ends? If not, they will not correctly identify our intellectual virtues. For starters, has Sosa identified an intellectual function that is specific to humans? Getting truths about one's surroundings doesn't seem unique to our species – most species need to get truths about, for instance, whether there are predators nearby. So, do other species also have some of the same intellectual virtues we have (e.g., reliable vision)? How important is it to identify intellectual ends and virtues that are specific to humans?

Let's assume that getting truths about our surroundings *is* one of our intellectual ends, even if it is not unique to us. Still, it isn't our only intellectual end. At minimum, avoiding falsehood is a second end; hence Sosa's emphasis on reliability – the production of *more* true beliefs than false ones. What other intellectual ends might we have? *Understanding* is a good candidate, and it might even be unique to us. Understanding a poem, a piece of music, or a theory may require having true beliefs about it. But, arguably, having true beliefs isn't sufficient for understanding. A student might memorize a piece of music, and even have a pile of additional true beliefs about it, but still fail to understand it. Something similar can be said of a theoretical proof, or even of one's best friend. Understanding your best friend involves more than having true beliefs about him or her. If understanding is an additional intellectual end, there will be additional virtues that attain it – Aristotle's and Sosa's lists of virtues may be too short.[11]

On the other hand, we might wonder whether Aristotle's list of intellectual ends and virtues is also too long. Why does "truth in agreement with right desire" count as an *intellectual* end, as opposed to a practical or moral end? Why does the *techne* involved in horsemanship count as an intellectual virtue, instead of a practical virtue? Why does *phronesis*, which requires possession of the moral virtues, count as an intellectual virtue, instead of a moral virtue?

Echoing the fifth objection at the end of section 2.1.1 (see page 43), do Aristotle and Sosa account for the value of the intellectual virtues? According to (TII), virtues get their value from the value of the ends they attain. That is, virtues are valuable insofar as they are means to, or parts of, *ends* that are valuable. So, is the intellectual end of getting truths valuable? The answer depends on whether all truths are valuable. Take contingent truths about our surroundings. There is a contingent truth about how many fibers are in your left sock right now. Is that truth valuable? Likewise, there is a contingent truth about what clothing Lindsay Lohan wore yesterday; and a contingent truth about the number of strikeouts Jared Weaver throws to left-handed batters on Tuesdays. Are those truths valuable? Why, or why not? Are they as valuable as truths about climate change, the economy, and ethics? Teleological notions of the good are silent about such matters. What we need is an independent account of which truths are, and which truths aren't, objectively valuable and why.

In more recent work, Sosa has taken steps toward such an account; and toward a nonteleological version of the first key concept of virtue. He has begun to replace arguments that truth is our function with arguments that at least some truths are intrinsically, or fundamentally, valuable (2003: 160; 2007: 72). He still argues that the intellectual virtues are instrumentally valuable as means to getting truths. But, he now thinks they are instrumentally valuable because they produce good epistemic *effects*, not because they attain an epistemic *end*. Moreover, he contends that the intellectual virtues are not *merely* instrumentally valuable; they are also constitutively and intrinsically valuable. Compare a person who gets truths because of good luck with a person who gets truths because of her intellectual virtues. Both get something of intrinsic, or fundamental, value – the truths in question. But, Sosa argues that the *way* the virtuous person gets truths has additional intrinsic value. Getting those truths is a credit to her; but not to the person who gets them because of luck (2003: 173–175; 2007: 88).

2.2 Virtues Attain Good Effects: The Nonteleological Variety

The nonteleological variety of the first key concept focuses on *effects*, rather than ends. Thus, it contends that virtues reliably succeed in getting good *effects*. Accordingly:

(NTI)   It defines virtues and vices in terms of effects; and
(NTII) It uses those effects to explain why virtues are valuable and vices are not.

According to (NTI), virtues just are qualities that enable a person or thing to reliably produce good effects. This means that to figure out which qualities are virtues, we need to determine which effects are good. Doing so is no easy matter. But, *if* truth and well-being are good effects, then reliable vision and benevolence will be virtues. According to (NTII), effects are what ultimately matter. Virtues derive their value from the value of the effects they produce. This means that to explain the value of the virtues, we need to explain the value of the effects. For instance, if truth and well-being are intrinsically valuable, then the virtues of reliable vision and benevolence will be (at minimum) instrumentally valuable since they are means to producing truth and well-being.

2.2.1 *Julia Driver*

Julia Driver explicitly rejects the teleological variety of the first key concept of virtue, but adamantly defends the non-teleological variety (2001: 96–97). She argues that a virtue is "a character trait that produces more good (in the actual world) than not systematically" (2001: 82). She distinguishes between two sorts of virtues: prudential virtues, which produce good effects for the person who has them; and moral virtues, which produce good effects for others. Her list of virtues includes: intelligence, genius, benevolence, courage, practical wisdom, modesty, wit, and even "sensitivity in administering [medical] treatment to children" (2001: 57).

Despite Driver's insistence that the virtues must be character traits, it appears that only some of the qualities she lists have that status (e.g., benevolence), while others are acquired skills (e.g., sensitivity in administering treatment to children), and still others are largely native capacities (e.g., intelligence). Driver's view is reminiscent of Hume's, both because it emphasizes the production of good consequences, and because it counts a wide range of qualities as virtues. Driver's and Hume's lists of virtues include moral qualities, intellectual qualities, qualities we voluntarily acquire, and involuntary qualities.

According to Driver, a quality counts as a virtue because it reliably produces good effects in normal conditions in the real world. Like Sosa, Driver thinks that virtues need not be perfect: they need not infallibly produce good effects; they need only produce a preponderance of good effects – *more* well-being than harm, *more* truth than falsehood. Driver and Sosa also agree that a quality's reliability is not impugned by its failure to produce good effects in unusual conditions. Imagine a person who, when confronted with highly unusual conditions – for example, Sophie in *Sophie's Choice* (1979) – does not know what do to. In Driver's words, "this does not mean that the agent lacks the relevant virtue [here, practical wisdom], any more than the fact that a fishing rod will break when run over by a steamroller means that it lacks the quality of resilience" (2001: 10–11). To be a virtue, a quality need only be disposed to reliably produce good effects in *normal* conditions. This means that virtues will be indexed to conditions. A quality – like honesty or benevolence – that reliably contributes to well-being in free societies ("normal" conditions), may produce far more harm than good in a society run by Nazis ("unusual" conditions).

Driver explicitly argues that good motives are not necessary for virtue. To illustrate, she contends that a doctor can fail to have good motives, but still have the virtue of sensitivity in administering treatment to children. In vaccinating children, this doctor may not care about the welfare of the child: "he may only be motivated by his income, or the esteem of his colleagues" (2001: 57). But, as long as he reliably succeeds in producing vaccinated and untraumatized children, he has the corresponding virtue.[12] In short, Driver thinks that reliably producing good effects is sufficient for virtue. Good motives are not needed. Reliably producing good effects is also necessary for virtue. Driver argues that "a well-intentioned person who habitually misses the good does not in fact have virtue. While her internal psychological states may be appropriate, she is failing to produce the good systematically" (2001: 70). For Driver, what happens in the world – the effects one produces – are what really matter. If one isn't reliably producing good effects, one doesn't have virtues.

Which effects does Driver think are good? Briefly, she thinks that the flourishing of oneself and others is good. Flourishing includes well-being and truth. On her view, moral virtues are qualities that contribute to "the flourishing of others . . . by helping to ease social interaction" (2001: 38). In short, moral virtues promote social good (2001: 74).

Objections

Spooked by ends and functions, the nonteleological variety avoids the objections given in the sections above. But, it still faces the daunting task of showing that some consequences are intrinsically valuable. Driver does not mount explicit arguments to that effect; she just assumes that if anything is intrinsically valuable, flourishing is. For Driver, the value of the virtues is derived from the value of the good effects they produce (2001: 63). So, the worry is that Driver won't be able to explain the value of the virtues until an account of the intrinsic value of flourishing (well-being, etc.) is provided.

Driver argues that virtues are dispositions to reliably produce good effects. Virtues do not require good motives, nor do they require knowledge of what is good. But, if they don't require features like motives or knowledge, what grounds the dispositions? *Something* must explain why a person is disposed to produce well-being (why she would produce well-being if given the opportunity). If it's not motives or knowledge that do the explaining, what does? Relatedly, if it's not motives or knowledge that do the explaining, what makes the virtues *character traits*, as opposed to skills or native capacities?

We might also worry that Driver makes virtues and vices too easy to get. On her view, virtues do not require good motives or knowledge of the good. Any trait that reliably produces good consequences counts as a virtue. Nor do vices require bad motives or false beliefs about the good. Any trait that reliably produces bad consequences counts as a vice. Accordingly, Driver is committed to the claim that Phineas Gage became vicious as a result of an accident that drove a metal bar through his frontal lobe (2001: 10).[13] Let's assume that, after the accident, Gage did indeed produce more harm than good. But, does that mean he was vicious? Or just sick and brain-damaged?

2.3   Luck in Getting Ends or Effects

Is there a difference between Doug, the failed doctor on *Scrubs*, and Gaylord Focker, the protagonist of the comedic film *Meet the Parents* (Universal, 2000), who is persistently beset by bad luck? And does this difference matter for virtue? Some philosophers think it does.

Let's compare the two. Doug clearly fails to produce good external ends or effects – he kills most of his patients. On a lesser scale, Focker also consistently fails to produce good external ends or effects. While visiting the home of his girlfriend's parents, he accidentally sets their yard on fire, breaks the nose of his girlfriend's sister, loses their cat, and destroys an urn which contains the ashes of their beloved grandmother. So, Doug and Focker have this much in common: neither of them produces good external ends or effects in the world. Still, there is an important difference between them: Doug doesn't even do what a good doctor would do. He doesn't perform the right actions – for example, he gives patients the wrong blood, the wrong medication, etc. In contrast, Focker often does what a good person would do – he often performs the right actions. He chases the cat that gets out (but causes a fire), opens a bottle of champagne to celebrate (but destroys the urn), and so on. So, arguably, Focker consistently fails to get good effects, not because he fails to do the right thing, but because of bad luck – he is surrounded by a world that doesn't go his way. (Nearly every comedic character played by Ben Stiller fits this mold.) On a more serious note, compare people who consistently fail to get good effects because they fail to do the right thing with people who do the right thing but have the bad luck of living in an oppressive society. The latter help others and tell the truth, but their helping and truth-telling consistently produces bad effects because they are surrounded by bad people. Imagine an innocent truth-teller incarcerated in San Quentin prison.

Some philosophers, like Julia Annas (2003) and Philippa Foot (1997), have argued that virtue does not require consistently attaining external ends or effects; but it does require consistently attaining internal goals. To explicate, they think there is a difference between consistently failing to achieve external effects because of internal psychological factors, and consistently failing to achieve external effects because of bad luck in the environment.[14] Annas and Foot argue that only the former impugns virtue. To illustrate: suppose that you are a disaster-relief surgeon, who is deployed to locations around the world in an effort to save victims of natural disasters. You care about saving these victims – in fact, you became a doctor because you care about others – but, even after years of service, you are still often initially shocked by the condition of the victims you see. And yet, you consistently perform the needed surgeries with tremendous skill, and do everything you can and should to save the victims in question. (You are *not* Doug.) In other words, you consistently attain your internal goal – you consistently overcome your initial shock, consistently do the right thing, and consistently do everything you can. But, the majority of the victims you perform surgery on still die, due to the severity of the disasters and the severity of their injuries. So, you consistently fail to attain your external goal of saving the victims, due to bad luck. Annas and Foot argue that we don't need to consistently attain external ends in order to have virtues. The disaster-relief surgeon doesn't need to consistently save her patients in order to have the virtue of benevolence. Here, the underlying intuition is that virtues are praiseworthy, and vices are blameworthy; and we should only be praised or blamed for things we can control, like our motives and actions. We should not be praised or blamed for

3
Motives Matter: Virtues Require Good Motives

In Chapter 1, we identified two key concepts of virtue. As we have seen, the first key concept claims that attaining good ends or effects is enough, and is required, for virtue. Good motives aren't needed. This chapter focuses on the second key concept, which claims that attaining good ends or effects is not enough for virtue, and may not even be required. It also matters *why* one attains, or tries to attain, good effects. In short, internal psychological features, like motives, matter; good motives are intrinsically valuable. And virtues matter, in part, because they involve good motives. In short, the second key concept makes two important claims:

(MI) It defines virtues and vices (at least partly) in terms of internal psychological features, like motives.
(MII) It uses those internal psychological features to (help) explain why virtues are valuable and vices are not.

According to the second key concept, good motives (or other good psychological features) are *necessary* for virtue. A person might produce loads of good effects in the world. But, if she does so for the wrong reasons or as a result of bad motives, then she isn't virtuous. To illustrate, recall the venture capitalist in Chapter 1, who consistently produces good effects by donating money to hospitals. Though he reliably succeeds in making the world a better place, his motives are selfish – he only cares about getting his name on buildings, not about the people who are helped. Hence, the second key concept maintains that he does not have the virtue of benevolence. Likewise, it maintains that scientists who reliably produce truths, but who are motivated by fame rather than by the discovery of truth itself, are not intellectually virtuous. Watson and Crick may fall into this category.[1] As may other reliable scientists, who are "obsessed with making a big splash and issuing press releases."[2]

This may sound odd. After all, if a person is already producing good effects in the world, isn't she already virtuous? Why do virtues require good motives? Advocates of the second key concept give us two reasons. First, they contend that virtues are praiseworthy and vices are blameworthy; and that we can't be legitimately praised or blamed for things that aren't under our control. For instance, a person can't be praised for his good eyesight, since he has no control over which hard-wired faculties he ends up with. Nor can he be blamed for his inability to empathize with others when it is the result of a developmental disability. For an agent to be praiseworthy for her virtues, or blameworthy for her vices, she must have a considerable degree of control over them. Arguably, we have significantly more control over our motivations and actions than we do over our effects in the outside world. If we have control over anything, it is our actions (at least some of them). We also have some control over whether we end up caring about other people, or only about our own reputations; and whether we end up caring about the truth, or only about the spotlight. Arguably, we have less control over our effects in the world, which are more susceptible to luck. Whether we succeed in producing good effects depends not just on us, but on the cooperation of the rest of the world. We must have the good luck of living in an hospitable environment – one that isn't controlled by dictators or omnipotent evil demons – an environment in which others don't prevent us from producing good effects. All of this means that good motives are required for virtues because virtues are praiseworthy, and good motives can legitimately be praised. Good effects can't, since they are more susceptible to luck. A Scrooge (pre-conversion), who happens to live in a world controlled by omnipotent angels, would produce good effects and be prevented from producing bad ones. But, he would produce good effects due purely to good luck.

Second, these philosophers contend that virtues and vices tell us who we are as individual people. In other words, a person's virtues and vices will express her character – they will reveal what she cares about and values. But, actions, good effects, and hard-wired capacities won't reveal what a person cares about or values. Consider actions. Two people who both donate money to hospitals may, nevertheless, do so for very different reasons: one because she cares about sick people, the other because he cares about his own reputation. Accordingly, actions themselves tell us relatively little about the person performing them. Something similar can be said of good effects. A person who consistently produces good effects may do so because of good luck – he may be a selfish misanthrope who happens to land in an angel-world. So, arguably, good effects are also limited in what they tell us about an individual's character. Hard-wired capacities are even more limited. After all, children and animals have hard-wired capacities, like vision, even though they don't (yet) have any values to speak of. In short, virtues and vices won't reveal what a person cares about and values, unless they include internal psychological features, like motives and beliefs. Accordingly, some philosophers argue that virtues require good motives and knowledge of the good, while vices require bad motives and false beliefs about the good.

Consequently, according to the second key concept, virtues are acquired character traits, rather than hard-wired capacities. They require motivations, and dispositions of action, that we acquire over time, via practice and effort. Do virtues also require attaining good ends or effects? Or, are good motives and good actions *sufficient* for virtue? Advocates of the second key concept disagree. Hence, this concept comes in two varieties: the motives-actions-and-ends variety, and the motives-actions-no-ends variety.

According to the motives-actions-and-ends variety, virtues require good motives, good actions, *and* reliable success in producing good ends or effects. Good motives and actions by themselves won't be enough, since virtuous people must also be effective. Here, internal psychological states, like motives, matter; but so do external effects. Accordingly, if a person consistently fails to produce good effects, then he doesn't have virtues; even if his motives and actions are impeccable. This means that, say, Malala Yousafzai won't have virtues unless she makes progress in improving girls' access to education in places like Pakistan. Arguably, Yousafzai (at age 16) already has stable dispositions to care about the welfare of girls and the poor, and already values education and equal access to it. She has also repeatedly defended her views, and criticized the Taliban, at enormous risk to herself – she was shot in the head by the Taliban in October 2012, while coming home from school in Mingora, Pakistan (Yousafzai 2013). So, Yousafzai already seems to have the motives and dispositions of action that are needed for virtues like courage, justice, and benevolence. But, according to the motives-actions-and-ends variety, she won't have those virtues unless she also produces a net gain of good external effects. Now, she need not produce them overnight; nor need she solve all of Pakistan's problems. She need only make some overall progress in improving girls' access to education. (Arguably, she already has.) To have virtues, she must, on balance, be effective. So, if Yousafzai's efforts at improving girls' access to education fail to make any actual progress, she doesn't have virtues. This will be so even if her efforts fail due to the bad luck of her political circumstances. As we will see below, Linda Zagzebski (1996) explicitly advocates the motives-actions-and-ends variety. Whether Aristotle and Rosalind Hursthouse (1999) also endorse it depends on how we interpret them.

In contrast, the motives-actions-no-ends variety claims that good motives and good actions (along with other good psychological states) will be sufficient for virtue. Reliably attaining good ends or effects is not required. Here, internal psychological states and dispositions of action are all that matter. Virtuous people need not be, on balance, externally effective. So, very roughly, if Yousafzai consistently cares about what she should – including girls' equal access to education – and consistently stands up for people who need help, and people who are being treated unfairly, then she will (arguably) have virtues like courage, justice, and benevolence.[3] She will have these virtues even if the Taliban prevents her from making any actual progress. According to the motives-actions-no-ends variety, bad luck in a person's circumstances (political or otherwise) doesn't detract from her character. James Montmarquet (1993) and Michael Slote (2001, 2010) both explicitly advocate this variety of the second key concept of virtue.

3.1 Virtues Require Good Motives-and-Actions, but Attaining Good Ends?

Aristotle and the contemporary ethicist Rosalind Hursthouse explicitly argue that moral virtues require good motives and good actions. Do they also think that moral virtues require attaining external ends or effects? That depends on how we interpret them.

3.1.1 *Aristotle:* Nicomachean Ethics *II*

Though Aristotle employs the first key concept of virtue in Books I and VI of *Nicomachean Ethics*, the second key concept is clearly the star of NE. In NE.II.6, Aristotle argues that a moral virtue is a "state of character concerned with choice, lying in a mean, the mean relative to us, this being determined by a rational principle, and by that principle by which the man of practical wisdom would determine it" (NE.1107a1–2). Let's unpack this definition. First, Aristotle thinks that moral virtues are *states of character* rather than natural faculties. He argues that natural faculties can't be moral virtues because virtues are praiseworthy, and we can't be "praised or blamed" for natural faculties, over which we have no control (NE.1106a8). We can, however, be praised for acquired states of character, like courage, temperance, and justice, since we have some control over their acquisition.

Second, he argues that even though skills (*techne*) are acquired, they are not moral virtues, since virtues require *choice* (*prohairesis*), but skills do not. On Aristotle's view, both virtues and skills require actions of some sort. But, unlike skills, virtues require us to "choose" the right actions, and choose them for their own sakes (NE.II.4). Aristotle's notion of choice is complicated. Roughly, when a person chooses an action for its own sake, she has a rational desire (*boulesis*) to perform the action. In other words, she wants to perform the action because she believes that the action is morally good. For Aristotle, the notion of rational desire combines reason with desire: in rationally desiring an action, a person wants to do what reason tells her is right. This means that to have rational desires, a person must have a conception of the moral good – she must have beliefs about what is good. Moreover, argues Aristotle, a virtuous person must have true beliefs (roughly, knowledge) about what is good – her conception must be correct.

So, why does virtue, but not skill, require choice and rational desire? On Aristotle's view, an agent's virtues express who she is as a person – they tell us what she cares about and values; they reveal her conception of the good. But, an agent's actions, on their own, won't tell us any of these things. After all, two adults can perform the very same action, but with different motives and conceptions of the good; and children can act well before they have developed conceptions of the good. This means that for virtues to express who we are as people, they must involve something besides actions – something that reveals our motives, commitments, values, and conceptions of the good. For Aristotle, that something is choice. So, virtues require choice and rational desire because virtues must tell us who we are as people. In contrast, skills do not require choice or rational desire because skills need not tell us who we are as people – they need not express our commitments and values. An adult can develop skills (in managing bureaucracy) that he believes to be a waste of time or skills (in military strategy) that he believes to be morally objectionable; and a child can develop skills (in gymnastics) well before she develops a conception of the moral good.

In short, Aristotle thinks that moral virtues require internal psychological features, like choice and rational desire. Action, by itself, won't be enough for virtue. Granted, to have the virtue of (say) courage, one must perform the same acts that a courageous person would perform. But, one must also perform them for the same reasons and motives – choosing them for their own sakes. So, for Aristotle, standing up to a bully won't be enough; one must also do so because one correctly believes that it is worth the risk. On his view, virtues are acquired dispositions of action, motivation, emotion, and perception. One must be disposed to: perform the right actions, from the right motives, have the right emotions, and see the world the right way. To illustrate, the courageous person must "face . . . and . . . fear . . . the right things . . . from the right motive, in the right way and at the right time . . ." (NE.1115b18–19). Which actions, motives, emotions, and so on, are *the right* ones?

Aristotle famously argues that each virtue *lies in a mean* between a vice of excess and a vice of deficiency. Thus, the virtue of courage lies in a mean between the vice of rashness, and the vice of cowardice. To illustrate, the protagonists of the film and television series *Jackass* are rash. For starters, they have too much confidence and not enough fear. They aren't afraid of being launched from catapults, but they should be. Moreover, they consistently face (indeed, generate) risks that they should avoid. At the other extreme, consider Sir Robin the Brave, a character in the film *Monty Python and The Holy Grail* (1975). Sir Robin is a coward. He has too much fear and not enough confidence – he is afraid of everything (his icon is a chicken). And he consistently runs away from risks that he should face. In contrast with both extremes, the courageous person "hits the mean" in her actions and emotions. She faces the risks she should, and avoids the risks she should; she feels fear when she should, and feels confidence when she should. In short, she performs the right actions, from the right motives, and has the right emotions and perceptions. Does this mean that the courageous person always feels a moderate amount of fear, no matter what the situation? It does not. Aristotle thinks that there are some contexts in which the courageous person is very afraid (e.g., on the battlefield), and other contexts in which she has no fear (e.g., when hanging out with friends). Does it mean that the courageous person always confronts risk, no matter what the situation? Again, it does not. Sometimes the risk is so great (e.g., a confrontation with an armed robber) that the courageous person runs away. On Aristotle's view, discretion sometimes is the better part of valor.

For Aristotle, the virtues are not canned responses. The courageous person doesn't always behave in the same way, or feel the same thing. (If she did, acquiring the virtue of courage would be much easier than it is.) To have the virtue of courage, one must do and feel what is appropriate to the context. Hence, Aristotle's claim that *the mean is relative to us*. This amounts to claiming that the mean is context-sensitive. For instance, in the context of asking one's boss for a much-deserved raise, one hits the mean by feeling some trepidation, but asking anyway; whereas in the context of being confronted by an armed robber, one hits the mean by feeling terrified and running away. Now, Aristotle is not a relativist. He does not think that *we*, however far we fall short of virtue, get to set a moving standard for what is right in any given context.[4] Rather, he is an objectivist. He thinks that for each context, there is a right action, motivation, emotion, and way of sizing it up; and, that this is *determined by the person of practical wisdom* – the ideally virtuous person.[5] It is not determined by the rest of us. The person of practical wisdom (the *phronimos*) has all of the moral virtues and *phronesis*, thus she knows what is best in every context (see 2.1.2 above). On Aristotle's view, it is the *phronimos* who sets the standard for which actions, motives, emotions, and perceptions are right in each context. Accordingly, one hits the mean in a context by doing, feeling, seeing, and being motivated by the same things as the *phronimos*. Aristotle ultimately argues that we can't do this without acquiring the moral virtues and *phronesis* ourselves – without becoming *phronimoi*. Consequently, Aristotelian virtues will be very difficult to acquire!

What makes Aristotelian virtues valuable? For starters, Aristotle clearly thinks that the virtues are *intrinsically* valuable. On his view, we choose the virtues "for themselves (for if nothing resulted from them we should still choose . . . them)" (NE.1097b2–3). In other words, he thinks the virtues are valuable for their *own* sakes – they are intrinsically valuable. He doesn't say exactly *what* makes them intrinsically valuable, but we can plausibly assume that choice, rational desire, and knowledge of the good all contribute to their intrinsic worth. Aristotle also clearly thinks that the virtues are valuable because they contribute to living well (happiness). In his words, we choose the virtues not just for themselves, but also "for the sake of happiness, judging that through them we shall be happy" (NE.1097b3–5). There are different ways in which the virtues might contribute to living well. They might be part of what it is to live well; or they might produce good lives, or parts of good lives; or both (see 1.2.2 above). Arguably, Aristotle thinks that the virtues do both. In NE.I, he contends that the virtues are an important part, but not the only part, of living well – the virtues are needed for living well, but so are other goods, like health, pleasure, and friendship (see Chapter 6 below). Accordingly, he thinks that the virtues are *constitutively* valuable because they are part of living well (which is the chief good). But, he also thinks that the virtues tend to produce benefits for the people who possess them – they tend to produce some of the other goods that are needed for living well, like pleasure and (perhaps) friendship. So, arguably, he also thinks that the virtues are often *instrumentally* valuable, insofar as they produce such goods.[6]

3.1.2 Rosalind Hursthouse

Rosalind Hursthouse is a self-avowed "neo-Aristotelian" (1999: 8). Like Aristotle, she argues that dispositions to have good motives are necessary for moral virtue. On her view, moral virtues are character traits: they are dispositions of action, motivation, emotion, and perception. The paradigms of moral virtue include benevolence, courage, temperance, and honesty. To illustrate, the person who has the virtue of honesty tends to act in particular ways: he tells the truth, he doesn't cheat, etc. But, according to Hursthouse, acting in these ways isn't sufficient for being honest – an agent's actions can make him *appear* honest even if he isn't. In her words:

> [O]ne can give the appearance of being [an] . . . honest . . .
> person without being one, by making sure one acts in certain
> ways. And that is enough to show that there is more to the
> possession of a virtue than being disposed to act in certain

ways; at the very least, one has to act in those ways for certain sorts of reasons. (1999: 11)

Like Aristotle, Hursthouse thinks that there is more to virtue than meets the eye. To have the virtue of honesty, we must not only tell the truth; we must do so for the right reasons. The person who tells the truth, but does so only because he would get caught lying, isn't honest. In short, Hursthouse thinks that to have the virtues, our reasons and motives must be good.[7] Internal psychological features, like reasons and motives, matter.

Exactly which internal psychological features are needed for moral virtue? In *On Virtue Ethics*, Hursthouse argues that virtue requires: knowledge, choice, and a correct conception of the good.[8] In this, she follows Aristotle (NE.II.4). To explicate, let's begin with knowledge. Hursthouse argues that to have a moral virtue, a person must *know* what she is doing and why she is doing it (1999: 124). Merely *doing* the same thing that a virtuous person would do isn't enough. After all, one might do the very thing that a virtuous person would do, but do it by accident, or at the behest of another person (as children do). To illustrate, Suzy might tell the truth, but do it by accident or because she is following someone else's instructions. When that happens, Suzy isn't praiseworthy for the actions she performs, since they are not due to her, but to luck or to someone else. To be praiseworthy for performing acts that are right (e.g., for telling the truth), a person must, at minimum, know what she is doing (she must know that she is telling the truth). Now, all the advocates of the second key concept of virtue, including Hursthouse, assume that, to have a virtue, a person must be praiseworthy for performing acts that are right. Hence, having virtue requires knowing what one is doing.

Second, Hursthouse argues that virtue also requires *choosing* the right acts for their own sakes (1999: 126). This means that telling the truth and knowing that you are telling the truth are still not enough for the virtue of honesty. To have the virtue of honesty, you must also "choose" to tell the truth for its own sake, in the Aristotelian sense. As we saw above, Aristotle's notion of choice requires rational desire (*boulesis*); roughly, in choosing to tell the truth for its own sake, you want to tell the truth because you believe it is good to do so. Specifically, argues Hursthouse, you want to tell the truth for the same reasons that an honest person wants to tell the truth. That is, you want to tell the truth because you believe that (say) listeners are entitled to the truth, or that it is best to get the truth out in the open, or that it is important to tell the truth even if it will be painful to hear. Hursthouse thinks that many of us have told the truth for reasons just like these; and that these reasons show that we have correct conceptions of the good. Accordingly, third, she thinks that virtue requires having true beliefs about what is good (1999: 136). These true beliefs need not be part of any fancy philosophical theory; they may simply be reasons like the ones above. This means that the honest person will know at least two things. Unlike Suzy, she will know that she is telling the truth. But she will also know, or at least have true beliefs, that telling the truth is good.

Together, the second and third psychological features constitute what Hursthouse calls "moral motivation." On her view, moral motivation is what distinguishes the people with genuine virtue from the fakers. Fakers might tell the truth, and know that they are doing so, but do so for the wrong reasons – they might (falsely) believe that telling the truth is bad, but do it because they don't want to get caught lying. To have the virtue of honesty, a person must tell the truth, know that she is telling the truth, and be morally motivated to do it.[9]

Like other Aristotelians, Hursthouse thinks that virtues are intrinsically valuable (1999: 108), and constitutively valuable (1999: 169) – valuable because they are the key part of living a good life. She also thinks that virtues usually (but not always) benefit the person who has them; they usually make that person's life good for him. They usually produce a life that is full of (e.g.) friendship and enjoyment. On her view, virtues are able to do this because they foster our basic human functions. In addition to being character traits that require moral motivation, virtues also enable us to live rationally (1999: 222). Hence, Hursthouse may also think that virtues are instrumentally valuable, insofar as they foster goods like friendship and enjoyment for the people who possess them.

3.1.3   Do Virtues Require Attaining Good Ends or Effects?

Clearly, Aristotle and Hursthouse think that moral virtues require good motives and good actions. Do they also think that moral virtues *require* attaining good ends or effects? Or, do they think that we can have moral virtues even if bad luck prevents us from reliably attaining good ends or effects? In short, are they in the motives-actions-and-ends camp, or the motives-actions-no-ends camp? Here, matters are much less clear. Some philosophers think that Aristotle falls in the motives-actions-and-ends camp. Thus, Daniel Russell claims that "on Aristotle's view, in order for an action to be virtuous, not only must it be done from the right internal states of the agent, but it must also succeed in hitting its external target" (2012: 125).[10] But, Julia Annas thinks that Aristotle is confused about whether the moral virtues require attaining external ends (2003: 26). Following the Stoics, Annas distinguishes between two ends: an internal overall end, or *telos*; and an external immediate end, or *skopos*. To illustrate: in running into a burning house to save his neighbor, Newark New Jersey Mayor Cory Booker (arguably) had two ends: the *skopos* of saving his neighbor; and the *telos* of living and acting virtuously. Booker attained both ends – he saved his neighbor, and acted virtuously. But, had a deranged gunman shot and killed his neighbor on the way out, bad luck would have prevented Booker from attaining his *skopos*, though not his *telos* – he still succeeded in acting virtuously (Annas 2003: 25). Annas argues that the virtues require attaining one's overall internal *telos*, but not one's immediate external *skopos*. She thinks Aristotle is of both minds on this issue. In sum, it appears that Aristotle could fall in either the motives-actions-and-ends camp or the motives-actions-no-ends camp, depending on how we interpret him. Perhaps, the same can be said of Hursthouse, though she seems to lean toward the motives-actions-no-ends camp. Hursthouse (1999: 94–99) expresses sympathy with Philippa Foot's (1997) suggestion that virtue should be insulated from bad luck in one's environment (see 2.3 above). So, she is likely to think that we can still have virtues, even if we have the bad luck of living in a world in which demons thwart our efforts to produce good effects.[11]

3.2 Virtues Require Good Motives-Actions-and-Attaining-Good-Ends: Linda Zagzebski

Linda Zagzebski is a contemporary epistemologist who bases her views about intellectual virtues on Aristotle's views about moral virtues. In *Virtues of the Mind*, she argues that a virtue is "a deep and enduring acquired excellence of a person, involving a characteristic motivation to produce a certain desired end and reliable success in bringing about that end" (1996: 137). Zagzebski applies this definition to moral virtues, like courage and benevolence, and intellectual virtues, like open-mindedness, and intellectual courage. Like Aristotle and Hursthouse, Zagzebski thinks that motives matter for virtue. She argues that virtues, whether moral or intellectual, are acquired character traits that require good motives and actions. But, unlike Aristotle and Hursthouse, she unambiguously falls in the motives-actions-and-ends camp. She explicitly argues that bad luck can prevent us from being virtuous: if we are in a demon-world in which all of our beliefs turn out to be false, then we don't have intellectual virtues, even if our motives are pristine.

Why does Zagzebski think that good motives are required for intellectual virtues? In contrast with Ernest Sosa, Zagzebski restricts intellectual virtues to character traits; that is, to "deep qualit[ies] of a person, closely identified with her selfhood" (1996: 104). Hence, she thinks that intellectual virtues cannot be subpersonal hard-wired faculties, like vision and memory, which most agents share with one another and with animals. On her view, such faculties lie entirely outside our control, and, more importantly, tell us nothing about who the individual agent is as a thinker. Instead, intellectual virtues must be acquired, praiseworthy qualities that tell us what the individual agent cares about (and values) in the intellectual realm. Likewise, intellectual vices will be acquired blameworthy qualities that tell us what the agent cares about (and values) in the intellectual realm. Accordingly, intellectual virtues and vices will tell us whether the agent cares about, for instance, truth and understanding, or believing whatever is easiest, or holding fast to her current beliefs come what may, or believing whatever will get published and make her famous.[12] Like Aristotle and Hursthouse, Zagzebski acknowledges that actions alone won't reveal any of this, since two agents can perform the same action for different reasons. To illustrate, suppose that in evaluating rough drafts of papers, a professor asks two students to consider alternative perspectives. Each student does so in her revisions, thus performing the same intellectual action. But, these actions, by themselves, don't reveal what the students care about or value. One student may have considered alternatives because she is genuinely interested in the topic and wants to get to the truth, while the other may have been going through the motions in order to improve her grade. Accordingly, on Zagzebski's view, dispositions of action aren't enough for virtue. For an intellectual quality to express what an agent cares about and values, it must include the agent's motives. And for such an intellectual quality to count as a virtue, rather than a vice, it must include good motives, like caring about truth.

Exactly which motives are good, and thus required for intellectual virtue? Zagzebski argues that each intellectual virtue involves two motivations. First, all of the intellectual virtues – open-mindedness, intellectual courage, etc. – share an underlying motivation for "cognitive contact with reality"; roughly, a motivation for truth, knowledge, and understanding (1996: 167). Second, Zagzebski thinks that this underlying motivation for truth generates the motives that are distinctive of each of the individual intellectual virtues. To illustrate, she thinks that agents who are motivated to get the truth will also be motivated to consider alternative perspectives – the motive that is distinctive of open-mindedness, since they will believe that considering alternatives is likely to lead to the truth. Likewise, such agents will also be motivated to persevere in their beliefs when faced with opposition – the motive distinctive of intellectual courage, since they will believe that persevering, until they are convinced otherwise, is likely to lead to the truth. In Zagzebski's words, "if a person is motivated to get the truth, she would be motivated to consider the ideas of others openly . . . not to back down too quickly when criticized, and all the rest" (1996: 176). To sum up, each intellectual virtue involves two motives. Open-mindedness involves the motive for truth and the motive to consider alternative ideas; intellectual courage involves the motive for truth and the motive to persevere in one's beliefs when faced with opposition; and so on. Zagzebski argues that the underlying motivation for truth, and the motives it generates, are all intrinsically valuable (1996: 202–209).

On Zagzebski's view, good motives aren't enough for intellectual virtue. Agents must also be disposed to perform appropriate intellectual actions, and to reliably get true beliefs. Intellectual actions are, roughly, actions we perform in conducting inquiries and acquiring beliefs; like, formulating hypotheses, searching for evidence, considering alternative perspectives, admitting mistakes, ignoring objections, jumping to conclusions, and so on. Some intellectual actions are appropriate, others are inappropriate. Many are invisible to observers. Zagzebski argues that each intellectual virtue requires a distinct disposition of action. Thus, open-mindedness requires agents to consider alternatives appropriately, intellectual courage requires agents to stand up for their beliefs appropriately, and so on. Merely being motivated to do these things isn't enough. To be, say, open-minded, one must also "actually be receptive to new ideas, examining them in an even-handed way" (1996: 177). One must, in Annas's words, attain one's internal *telos*. To illustrate, Zagzebski thinks that to be open-minded a person must actually consider appropriate alternatives and ignore inappropriate alternatives. She must "hit the mean" in her actions. Suppose Jane is an open-minded police detective who is investigating the homicide of a prostitute in New York. In forming a belief about the identity of the murderer, she will consider appropriate alternatives, each of which has a high probability of being true (the victim's employer, or one of her clients, did it). She will not consider inappropriate alternatives that are highly likely to be false (the Prime Minister of Canada did it). Nor will she ignore alternatives that are highly likely to be true (Battaly 2008). In contrast, a dogmatic person would consider too few alternatives – ignoring some that are likely to be true; while a "naive" person would consider too many alternatives – entertaining some that are likely to be false.

Zagzebski also explicitly argues that intellectual virtues require reliable truth-production. This unambiguously places her in the motives-actions-and-ends camp. On her view, if an agent has good motives and performs appropriate actions, but has the bad luck of being in a demon-world in which all of her beliefs turn out to be false, then she isn't intellectually virtuous. For Zagzebski, motives matter, but so do effects. Virtues require reliably producing good effects like true beliefs, or well-being; they require attaining one's external *skopos*. Zagzebski thinks this applies to both moral and intellectual virtues. In her words, "it does seem to me to be a plain fact about the way we ordinarily think of virtue that a virtuous person is someone who not only has a good heart but is successful in making the world the sort of place people with a good heart want it to be" (1996: 100). Hence, on her view, benevolent people are reliably successful in alleviating suffering; open-minded people are reliably successful in getting true beliefs; and so on. So, to sum up the above, Zagzebski's virtue of open-mindedness requires: (1) the motivation to get truths; (2) the motivation to consider alternative perspectives appropriately; (3) the disposition to actually consider the appropriate alternatives; and (4) the reliable production of true beliefs.

For Zagzebski, what makes intellectual virtues valuable? In *Virtues of the Mind*, she suggests that the intellectual virtues are intrinsically, constitutively, and instrumentally valuable. They are intrinsically valuable insofar as the motivation for truth is intrinsically valuable. On Zagzebski's view, we have good reason to think that the motivation for truth is intrinsically valuable. After all, she argues, we criticize agents who lack sufficient motivation for the truth, even when they get the truth (1996: 203–207). To illustrate, if Detective Jane (above) guessed the identity of the murderer instead of conducting an investigation, we would criticize her lack of motivation to get the truth; and we would do so even if she was lucky and guessed correctly. Zagzebski also suggests that the intellectual virtues are constitutively valuable in the same way that the moral virtues are – all the virtues are parts of living well. Finally, she implies that the intellectual virtues are instrumentally valuable insofar as they produce goods, like true beliefs.

3.3 Virtues Require Good Motives-and-Actions-but-not-Attaining-Good-Ends: Montmarquet and Slote

James Montmarquet and Michael Slote both clearly fall in the motives-actions-no-ends camp. Like Zagzebski, Montmarquet bases his analysis of intellectual virtue on Aristotle's analysis of moral virtue. But, unlike Zagzebski, he unambiguously falls in the motives-actions-no-ends camp. Montmarquet and Zagzebski agree that intellectual virtues are acquired character traits, over which we have some control, and for which we can thus be praised. As Montmarquet puts the point: "I [am] . . . interested in . . . qualities of intellectual character whose exercise is subject to our control . . . [and] for whose exercise or nonexercise we can properly be blamed or credited" (1993: 34). Montmarquet thinks that we have far more control over our motivations and actions than we do over our effects in the world, which depend a great deal on luck. Hence, he argues that intellectual virtues require dispositions of motivation and action, but do not require reliable truth-production. Motives and actions matter for virtue; effects do not.

On Montmarquet's view, intellectual virtues require an appropriate motivation to get truths and avoid falsehoods. This motivation is acquired rather than hard-wired, since many of us lack it. When the going gets tough, many of us ignore countervailing evidence and difficult questions; we care more about believing what we want than about believing the truth. In short, whatever hard-wired motivation we do have for the truth is often too weak. Montmarquet also thinks that, on some occasions, our motivation to get the truth can be too strong – some of us are "epistemic fanatics" (1993: 22). Accordingly, he argues that we must learn to care appropriately about the truth – roughly, we must learn to "hit the mean"; to care about the truth neither too little nor too much. Since we have some control over whether we develop this motivation (we can work at it), we merit praise when we do develop it. (Zagzebski agrees with all of this.)

Montmarquet identifies a primary intellectual virtue – conscientiousness – and three kinds of "regulating" intellectual virtues – the virtues of impartiality, sobriety, and intellectual courage. He thinks that conscientiousness is wholly constituted by the motivation to get truths. As we have seen, this motivation can be too weak or too strong. Accordingly, Montmarquet argues that an agent can be conscientious, while failing to be intellectually virtuous overall. For instance, an agent may fervently seek the truth, but also emphatically believe that she already has it. This agent is conscientious but dogmatic (1993: 22). To prevent conscientiousness from producing dogmatism, enthusiasm, and intellectual cowardice, Montmarquet argues that we need the regulating virtues of impartiality, sobriety, and intellectual courage. These regulating virtues involve additional motivations, and dispositions of action. All of these virtues work together in the agent to make her motivation for truth appropriate, and to make her intellectually virtuous overall. To illustrate: the virtue of open-mindedness (impartiality) involves the motivation to consider unfamiliar ideas, and the disposition to actually do so. Hence, the person who is both conscientious and open-minded is motivated to get truths and to consider unfamiliar ideas. She also succeeds in considering unfamiliar ideas when she should – she performs the right intellectual actions. Thus, the additional motivations and actions that are supplied by open-mindedness prevent the conscientious agent from drifting into dogmatism.

Montmarquet argues that although the intellectual virtues require appropriate motivations and actions, they do not require reliable truth-production. This squarely places him in the motives-actions-no-ends camp. On his view, intellectual virtues are widely believed to be reliable, and may even be reliable in the real world. But, they do not *require* reliability. In this manner, Montmarquet denies what Ernest Sosa (see 2.1.2 above) and Linda Zagzebski assert. To illustrate: for Montmarquet, a person will be open-minded whenever she has: (1) the motivation to get truths, (2) the motivation to consider unfamiliar ideas, and (3) the disposition to actually consider the unfamiliar ideas that she should. She need not produce a preponderance of true beliefs as a result. She can be massively deceived and still have the intellectual virtues. Why? Because, on Montmarquet's view, the bad luck of landing in a demon-world should not impugn her intellectual virtues. Suppose that, unbeknownst to us, a demon has manipulated our world so that true beliefs are, and have always been, best attained by the traits we call vices (e.g., dogmatism) rather than by the traits we call virtues (e.g., open-mindedness). Montmarquet argues that, were we to discover this, we would *not* conclude that "these apparent vices [e.g., dogmatism] are and have always been virtues"; nor would we conclude that "Galileo should . . . be regarded as epistemically vicious and, say, Schmalileo, his lazy, intellectually uncurious brother, as epistemically virtuous" (1993: 20). The open-mindedness of Galileo would still count as an intellectual virtue, even if it produced false beliefs; and the dogmatism of Schmalileo would still count as an intellectual vice, even if it produced true beliefs. Why? Because landing in a demon-world is purely a matter of bad luck, beyond the agent's control. Accordingly, it should not reflect negatively on the agent's intellectual character. In arguing the same point, Jason Baehr contends: "reliability is largely a matter of luck. Whether a person is successful at reaching the truth often depends, not just on her own motivation or 'best efforts,' but also on factors that are largely, if not entirely, outside her control – for example, the relative epistemic friendliness or hostility of her environment" (2011: 123). According to Baehr, it is a mistake to think that an agent's intellectual virtue "might depend on whether she is lucky enough to have the cooperation . . . of her environment. Rather . . . what seems relevant are certain 'internal' or psychological factors" (2011: 97). In sum, for Montmarquet and Baehr, motives (and actions) are what matter for intellectual virtue. Reliability is not required, since it is largely outside the agent's control.

Michael Slote is the leading advocate of the motives-actions-no-ends view of *moral* virtues. Slote argues that dispositions to have good motives, and perform good actions, are necessary and sufficient for moral virtue. On his view, we don't need to produce good external effects to have moral virtues; good motives and good actions are enough, even if they produce bad effects. In this manner, Slote affirms what Julia Driver denies (see 2.2.1 above).

Slote and Montmarquet share the intuition that virtues are internal states of agents – stable dispositions – that are praiseworthy; they are a credit to the agent who has them. On Slote's view, we can only be praised or blamed for things we can control. We can't be praised or blamed for things that result from luck, since such things do not reflect any credit or discredit on *us* as agents. In his words: "our common-sense moral intuitions find it implausible [that] . . . serious moral differences between people should be a matter of luck or accident, beyond anyone's control" (2001: 11).

This intuition grounds Slote's claim that good external effects are not necessary for virtue. Like Montmarquet, Slote thinks that our dispositions to produce good (or bad) effects in the world depend too much on luck, and too little on us. After all, good external effects can be due to good luck. For instance, greed and selfishness can "unintentionally produce good results" (2001: 120). Likewise, bad external effects can be due to bad luck. Due to no fault of our own, our well-planned charitable donations may end up in the hands of dictators who use them to do harm (2010: 134). But if this is so, then we can't (or, at least, can't consistently) be praised or blamed for our dispositions to produce effects in the world. Bad effects need not reflect any discredit on the agent – she may have done her best. Likewise, good effects need not reflect any credit on the agent – they may be due simply to good luck. Accordingly, Slote infers that bad effects do not count against an agent's moral worth or virtue. Nor do good effects count toward an agent's moral worth or virtue. Good and bad effects may only tell us about the agent's environment, they need not tell us anything about who she is as a person.

The intuition above also grounds Slote's claim that dispositions to have good motives, and perform good actions, are necessary for virtue. Like Montmarquet, Slote thinks we have considerably more control over our motives and actions than we do over our effects in the world. Accordingly, adults can be praised for developing good motives and performing good actions, and blamed for falling short: "a person can be morally criticized if she or her actions fail to exemplify a certain sort of balanced motivation" (2001: 90). That is, failing to have good motives reflects discredit on the agent, and counts against her virtue; while having good motives reflects credit on the agent, and counts toward her virtue. For Slote, motives matter for moral virtue.

In fact, for Slote, motives matter more than anything else – good motives are what make the virtues valuable. Slote argues that good motives are intrinsically, or fundamentally, valuable; they are "approvable in themselves" (2001: 38). Accordingly, the virtues are intrinsically valuable because they are largely comprised of good motives. According to Slote's "agent-based" virtue theory, good motives are also what make actions right: "an act is morally acceptable if and only if it comes from good or virtuous motivation" (2001: 38). Here, the key point is that virtues get their value from good motives, rather than from effects or actions (actions also get their value from good motives).

So, which motives are good? Slote focuses on a single good motive: empathic caring. He argues that not all caring is good. For instance, we often care far too much about ourselves and our own friends and families, and far too little about people we do not know. For caring to be good, we must strike a balance between caring about ourselves, about our own friends and families, and about people we don't know. Slote thinks that we can do this by improving our abilities to empathize with strangers. According to Slote, empathy is a capacity to have "the feelings of another (involuntarily) aroused in ourselves" (2010: 15). He argues that if we improve our capacities to empathize with people we don't know, then we will also develop the motivation to care about those people. To illustrate: if we improve our capacities to feel what girls who have been denied an education by the Taliban are feeling, then we will also develop the motivation to care about those girls. Empathic caring is the balanced motivation – to care about ourselves, our friends, and strangers – that results from improving our empathic abilities.

Is empathic caring the only good motive? Interestingly, Slote opts for a virtue ethics that "bases all morality" on the value of empathic caring (2001: 23). He considers, and rejects, two other motives. He rejects the "cool" motive of inner strength on the grounds that it cannot serve as the source of all moral value.[13] Second, he rejects the "warm" motive of universal benevolence because it is impartial – it requires us to care equally about each person, whether he or she is our child, parent, friend, or a stranger. In contrast, empathic caring is partial – it allows us to care more about some people than about others, though it does not allow our care for our intimates to dwarf our care for strangers.

Does Slote think characters like Mr. Bean and Doug from *Scrubs* are virtuous? After all, Mr. Bean and Doug appear to care about other people, and often try to help them. But, their efforts consistently end in comedic disaster. They are bunglers. Are they still virtuous? Slote thinks that since people like Bean and Doug can be morally criticized, they are *not* virtuous. They can be criticized on two related grounds. First, their actions can be criticized. Bean and Doug are negligent – neither bothers to figure out how to make his attempts at helping others successful. Neither makes any effort to "know [the] relevant facts" (2001: 105). Each performs the wrong actions again and again, when he could have easily determined which actions would have helped others. On Slote's view, caring just enough about others to try to help them isn't sufficient for virtue because it isn't sufficient for acting well. To be virtuous, one's actions must be good. Second, Bean and Doug can be criticized for their motives. For Slote, caring just enough about others to try to help them is not sufficient for *genuinely* caring about them – that is, for having a good motive. Slote thinks that people who genuinely care about others will make every effort to determine how best to act. Negligent actions like Bean's and Doug's demonstrate that they don't *really* care enough about other people – they don't have good motives. To further illustrate, suppose two people hear about the plight of girls in Taliban-controlled regions. One Googles "girls education Taliban," and donates money to the first website she sees, without bothering to read it closely. It turns out that the website is owned by an individual who opposes education for girls; and she would have discovered that had she read it closely. In contrast, the second person makes every effort to determine how best to help. Suppose that, after thorough research, he decides to donate money to a charity that has an excellent record of success. And yet, in an unprecedented move, the Taliban manages to seize the money raised by the website. Both these people end up producing bad effects. Like Bean and Doug, the former can be morally criticized for acting carelessly and for not caring enough. Unlike Bean and Doug, the latter cannot. He performed the right actions and had good motives. He did everything he could – his donation caused bad effects due simply to bad luck. Slote thinks that the former person is not virtuous, but the latter is. Like Montmarquet, Slote insulates virtue from this kind of bad luck.

3.4 Objections

First, should bad luck prevent us from being virtuous, as Zagzebski claims? Or, should virtue be impervious to luck, as Montmarquet and Slote claim? In short, should we join the motives-actions-and-ends camp, or the motives-actions-no-ends camp? The answer depends on how seriously we should take luck in the environment. This is a matter of heated debate in ethics and epistemology.

Montmarquet and Slote take luck seriously. They think that whether we reliably produce good effects in the world – true beliefs, well-being – is largely a matter of luck; and that bad luck cannot prevent us from being virtuous. But, we might worry that Montmarquet and Slote take luck *too* seriously. Granted, they are right that it is *possible* for bad luck to prevent us from reliably producing good effects; demon-worlds and Nazi societies are possible, and the latter are sometimes actual. But, the worry is that they aren't very *likely* or common – they are the exception, rather than the norm. In ordinary circumstances, demons and bad people aside, we often have control over whether we produce good effects in the world. To illustrate: I have control over whether I end up with true beliefs about the course grades my students have earned. I can keep track of the course grades, and double-check them and my grading formula. If I end up with false beliefs about my students' grades, I can and should be blamed – ending up with false beliefs counts against *me* and my character. In denying that reliability is required for intellectual virtue and thus insulating virtue from the threat of demon-worlds, Montmarquet's view pays a price. It sells our ordinary circumstances short – it undervalues the intuition that we often have control over whether we end up with true beliefs; that is, it undervalues the intuition that ending up with false beliefs often counts against *us*. Arguably, something similar can be said of Slote's view. Does this mean that we should side with Zagzebski – should we claim that the virtues require the reliable production of good effects?

Not necessarily, since we might worry that Zagzebski doesn't take luck seriously *enough*. Zagzebski's view, like Driver's and Sosa's, has the advantage of tying the agent's virtue to the outside world, and of making the agent's worth at least partly dependent on the effects she produces. These views can easily account for the intuition that I lack intellectual virtue, when I consistently produce false beliefs in circumstances that are under my control. But, Zagzebski, Driver, and Sosa also claim that an agent who produces bad effects, in circumstances that are *not* under her control, lacks virtue. And this is where we may balk. We may think that such views don't take the bad luck of landing in a demon-world seriously enough. We may think that Zagzebski undervalues the intuition that we should only be praised or blamed for things we can control. After all, why should the bad luck of being in a demon-world count against *us* and our character, when we can't control it? Shouldn't having good motives and performing good actions be enough for virtue, when we are stuck in an inhospitable environment due to no fault of our own?

In short, the jury is still out on how seriously we should take luck; and on which (if any) camp we should join. Perhaps we should consider a second key concept of virtue that accounts for both of the above intuitions. There may well be a middle ground between the motives-actions-and-ends view, on the one hand, and the motives-actions-no-ends view, on the other. We would do well to explore this middle ground; roughly, a motives-actions-and-*some-ends-but-not-others* view. This view would distinguish circumstances we can control from circumstances we can't.[14]

Second, what about (MII) – the claim that motives, and other psychological features, explain why the virtues are valuable? All the philosophers discussed above think that the virtues, whether moral or intellectual, are intrinsically valuable. But, interestingly, we get relatively little argument for this claim; and the arguments we do get are incomplete. Thus, Aristotle and Zagzebski both argue that the virtues are intrinsically valuable on the grounds that we do in fact value them, even when they don't produce good effects.[15] But, the mere fact that we do value something, x, independently of its effects does not entail that x really is intrinsically valuable. We could be mistaken – we could believe that x is intrinsically valuable, when it isn't. At best, the fact that we do value virtues, independently of their effects, serves as an inductive indicator that the virtues are intrinsically valuable, not a deductive proof. Slote (like Zagzebski) explicitly locates the intrinsic value of the virtues in the intrinsic value of motives. But, it is not clear why Slote restricts intrinsic value to a single kind of motive: empathic caring. How is a "warm" motive like empathic caring supposed to explain the value of virtues like courage and temperance? Wouldn't a "cool" motive like inner strength be better suited for this task? Why doesn't the motive of inner strength *also* count as intrinsically valuable? In Chapter 2.2, we saw Driver struggling to explain which things are intrinsically valuable and why. Many philosophers who endorse the second key concept have done no better.[16] Arguing for the intrinsic value of anything has proven to be difficult. Often, what we get are promissory notes.

Third, given the descriptions of the moral and intellectual virtues above, we might wonder whether any of us ever possesses the virtues. After all, they are difficult to get. They require acquired motivations, consistent patterns of action (which we must also learn over time), and, on Aristotle's view, hitting the mean. Arguably, hitting the mean requires possession of all the moral virtues and practical wisdom. But, who has all of that? Accordingly, the second key concept of virtue encounters the opposite problem from the first key concept. Whereas virtues, as described by the first key concept, are too easy to get, so virtues, as described by the second key concept, are too hard.

Situationists, like John Doris and Gilbert Harman, agree. Doris (2002) argues that most of us lack the virtues, as described above; and Harman (1999) suggests that such virtues may not even exist. After all, the second key concept claims that virtues are global – virtues require patterns of action (motivation, etc.) that are consistent across diverse conditions or 'situations'. But, according to Doris and Harman, when we look at the real world, we don't find patterns of action that are consistent across diverse situations. Instead, we find that in trivially different situations, people perform *different* actions. Thus, Doris and Harman argue that in some situations (e.g., when in a good mood, when early, when alone), we help the people we should; but in other trivially different situations (e.g., when in a bad mood, when running late, when in a group), we don't help the people we should. Since the virtue of benevolence requires helping the people we should across *all* these situations, Doris concludes that most people lack global virtues, like benevolence, and that concepts of global virtue should be eliminated from ethics (2002: 108). Harman goes even farther, concluding that there may be "no such thing as character" and that "there is no empirical basis for the existence of character traits" (1999: 316).

To explicate, Doris and Harman employ several studies in social psychology, including John Darley and Daniel Batson's good samaritan experiment (1973), and Stanley Milgram's famous obedience experiments (1974). In the good samaritan experiment, Princeton seminarians were first asked to complete questionnaires, and were then told that they had to give a speech in a different building on campus. Some were told that they were running late for the speech; others that they were a bit early; and others that they were on time. On their way across campus, all the seminarians encountered a person (an experimental confederate) who was clearly suffering from distress. Darley and Batson found that only 10 percent of the seminarians who were "late" stopped to help. By comparison, 63 percent of those who were "early," and 45 percent of those who were "on time," stopped. In Milgram's experiments, subjects were instructed to "shock" a person (a confederate) each time he made a mistake. Subjects were told that with each new mistake, the intensity of the "shock" increased (from a slight shock to a shock labeled "XXX"). Unbeknownst to subjects, the shocks weren't real. Confederates played their parts well, screaming in agony and pleading to be released from the experiment. As a result, many subjects expressed concern; but they were instructed to continue. Milgram found that, despite the screams and pleas of confederates, approximately 65 percent of subjects administered all the shocks; 35 percent refused at some point along the line. Presumably, the subjects who administered all the shocks did *not* routinely harm others in their ordinary lives – they weren't consistently cruel. But, they did "harm" others when instructed to do so by an experimenter. According to Doris, these studies show that most of us lack the consistent pattern of action that is required for the global virtue of benevolence. Most of us only help people in distress in specific types of situations – for example, when we aren't late for an appointment. Even more chilling, most of us will "harm" others in specific types of situations – when an experimenter tells us to do so. Doris concludes that most of us lack global character traits, like benevolence. At best, he thinks we have "local" traits, like "being-early-benevolence," whose patterns of action are consistent within a specific type of situation, but not across diverse situations.

We will revisit situationism in Chapter 7. In the meantime, suppose that most of us do fall short of fully possessing the virtues. How much does this matter? According to Hursthouse, it may not matter much, especially if we come close. Hursthouse argues that many of us are fairly, but not fully, virtuous: we are generally "quite honest, just, generous, [and] temperate"; we can typically be counted on to perform the right acts from the right motives. But, we also have minor "blindspots" that prevent us from being fully virtuous (1999: 150). For instance, someone might "lie about their forebears, but nothing else" (1999: 149); or overindulge, but only when visiting Las Vegas. (These agents are closer to full virtue possession than the subjects above.) Hursthouse thinks that even if most of us fall short of fully possessing the virtues, the ideally virtuous agent still sets the standard against which we are measured – a standard toward which we get closer. Chapter 4 explores ways in which we can fall short of full virtue possession, without possessing vices.

4
Vice and Failures of Virtue

Together, the previous chapters have argued that a person can be excellent in a variety of ways: she can be excellent insofar as she has good vision, or insofar as she is skilled at logical problem solving, or insofar as she is open-minded, courageous, or benevolent. Each of these qualities is a virtue. Some of them are virtues because they consistently attain good ends or effects (the first key concept); others are virtues because they involve good motives (the second key concept). Many of us fail to have virtues. Sometimes we fail because we have vices. Just as virtues are excellences, so vices are defects. Analogously, we should expect that a person can be defective in a variety of ways: she can be defective insofar as she has bad vision, or insofar as she makes systematic errors in logic, or insofar as she is dogmatic, cowardly, or cruel. As we will see below, each of these qualities is a vice. Some of them are vices because they consistently attain bad ends or effects; others are vices because they involve bad motives. Just as there are two key concepts of virtue, so there are two key concepts of vice.

Let's begin with patently clear illustrations of these two different kinds of vice. Adolf Hitler (1889–1945) clearly had the vice of cruelty. During World War II, Hitler and the Nazi Party intentionally and systematically enslaved, tortured, and exterminated approximately eleven million people. Six million of those exterminated were Jews. Many others were Romani, disabled, or homosexual. Hitler's motives were racist, anti-Semitic, and homophobic. He and the Nazi leadership wanted to rid Europe, and the world, of humans they believed to be "inferior." Their genocide of the Jews was deliberate – it was part of their plan to "purify" the world of "inferior" races. Clearly, Hitler's motives were bad, his beliefs were false, his actions were bad, and he produced horrific atrocities. He was blameworthy for all of this. This sort of vice is addressed in section 4.2.1 below.

Now, let's consider a very different kind of vice: bad vision. A person with uncorrected 20/200 vision will have far more false, than true, beliefs about her surroundings. Without eyeglasses, she will have so many false beliefs about the objects in her environment that she may have difficulty getting around. In the United States, the standard for legal blindness is 20/200 vision *with* correction. Bad vision produces bad effects – false beliefs. But, unlike cruelty, bad vision is hard-wired. We have no control over whether we end up with it, and consequently, are not blameworthy for it. This sort of vice is addressed in section 4.1 below.

One way to fall short of virtue is to have vice. Are there other ways to fall short of virtue? Could we fall somewhere in between having a virtue and having a vice? Let's consider two examples. First, suppose your best friend, call him Bill, constantly cheats on his partner Hilary. Bill and Hilary have agreed to have an exclusive relationship. Moreover, Bill knows that it is bad to cheat on Hilary, and wants to honor his commitment to Hilary. But, Bill cheats anyway, because he also wants the pleasure of sex with other people. You know Bill well. You know that he isn't sick: he does not have a pathological sexual addiction; he is just making bad choices, for which he is blameworthy. To his credit, Bill knows that he shouldn't have sex with other people, and feels awful about it after the fact. Nevertheless, he continues to cheat. Does Bill have a vice? On the one hand, Bill's actions are bad, and some of his motives are bad (he wants to have sex with other people). He is blameworthy on both counts. But, on the other hand, some of his motives are good, and he knows what he should do, even though he cannot get himself to actually do it. Section 4.3 addresses whether Bill has a vice.

Second, imagine that considering alternative points of view is a struggle for you. You know that you are more likely to get true beliefs if you consider different perspectives. In short, you know that you should be seeking out reasonable alternatives and objections to your ideas. And, eventually, you get yourself to do it. But, in the process, you have to overcome competing motivations to ignore ideas that are different from your own. You may undergo struggles like this in arriving at beliefs about religion and politics. Do you have a virtue? On the one hand, you know what you should do, and eventually succeed in doing it – your actions are good. (You differ from Bill, above, whose actions are bad.) But, on the other hand, you also have competing motives, and have to work hard to do the right thing. Section 4.4 addresses whether those of us who struggle still have virtue.

4.1　Ends Matter: Vices Attain Bad Ends or Effects

Chapter 2 argued that one way to be virtuous is to attain good ends or effects. Analogously, one way to be vicious is to attain *bad* ends or effects. According to the first key concept of virtue and vice, ends or effects are what ultimately matter. It is intrinsically good to have true beliefs, and to help others; it is intrinsically bad to have false beliefs, and to harm others. Accordingly, qualities that produce good ends or effects are excellences; and qualities that produce bad ends or effects are defects. Just as virtues get their positive value from the intrinsically good ends they produce, vices get their negative value from the intrinsically bad ends they produce. In short, vices just are qualities that reliably produce the bad.

So, according to the first key concept of vice, reliably producing the bad is both necessary and sufficient for vice. Thus, a king who intends to harm his subjects, but consistently bungles the job, producing their welfare instead, does not have the vice of cruelty. Similarly, a person who wants to believe whatever is easiest, but has the good luck of being in a world in which all her beliefs turn out to be true, does not have intellectual vices. To be a vice, a quality *must* produce bad effects. Those bad effects are what give vices their negative value. Having bad motives is not enough.

Reliably producing the bad is also *sufficient* for vice. Any quality that reliably produces the bad will count as a vice, whether the quality is a hard-wired faculty like vision, an acquired "anti-skill" like affirming the consequent, or an acquired character trait like cruelty. So, the king who intends to help his subjects, but, being in a world controlled by evil demons, consistently harms them instead, has the vice of cruelty. Likewise, the logic student who tries hard to get true beliefs, but still reliably gets false ones, has epistemic vices, like the vice of affirming the consequent. In sum, one way for a person to be defective is to have a quality that consistently produces bad ends or effects in the external world. Such qualities make us defective, even if our motives and psychologies are exemplary.

Julia Driver explicitly endorses this concept of vice. She argues that, just as virtues are qualities that consistently produce good effects, vices are qualities that consistently produce bad effects, like harm and falsehood. In her words: "vices . . . produce bad states of affairs" (2001: 74). For Driver, any stable quality that produces bad effects will count as a vice. Bad motives are not required. Accordingly, Driver's list of vices will be broad, including qualities like cruelty and cowardice (acquired character traits), insensitivity in administering treatment to children (an acquired "anti-skill"),[1] and dumbness (which may be largely innate). Driver thinks that vices need not be blameworthy. Consider Phineas Gage. In mid-nineteenth-century Vermont, a construction accident drove an iron rod through Gage's brain. As a result, he lost his ability to make moral decisions – he became untrustworthy. On Driver's view, Gage was not blameworthy for being untrustworthy, but his untrustworthiness was still a vice. It was a vice because it produced bad effects – Gage could not be trusted to do the right thing (2001: 10).

Similarly, nobody is blameworthy for having bad (20/200) vision. We have no control over the presence or absence of hard-wired faculties like bad vision. But, bad vision is still a vice because it produces bad effects – false beliefs. Ernest Sosa counts bad vision as an intellectual vice. Sosa implies that just as intellectual virtues are qualities that reliably produce true beliefs, intellectual vices are qualities that reliably produce false beliefs.[2] On his view, bad vision is a defective quality – a vice – because it is unreliable: it produces far more false, than true, beliefs. Other intellectual vices include: bad memory, color-blindness, guessing, ignoring contrary evidence, wishful thinking, and crystal-ball gazing. Sosa also implies that unreliability is necessary and sufficient for intellectual vice. He thinks that a person who wants to believe whatever is easiest, but has the good luck of being in a world in which all her beliefs turn out to be true, does not have intellectual vice; while a person who has exemplary motives, but has the bad luck of being in a demon-world in which all her beliefs turn out to be false, does have intellectual vice.[3]

In a similar vein, Miranda Fricker implies that testimonial injustice is a vice because of the bad effects it produces. In her innovative *Epistemic Injustice* (2007), Fricker contends that racial and gender prejudices in society infect our perceptions of who is credible and who is not. To illustrate, she argues that in the film *The Talented Mr. Ripley* (Miramax, 1999), gender prejudice prevents Herbert Greenleaf from seeing Marge as a source of knowledge about his son's disappearance (Fricker 2007: 87–88). Like Greenleaf, we have the vice of testimonial injustice when our perception of who is, and who is not, credible is prejudiced and unreliable. Fricker thinks that we cannot avoid inheriting such prejudice from society; and, thus, are not blameworthy for it. Such prejudice can operate unconsciously, even when we are deliberately motivated to end racial and gender injustice. So, bad motives are not what make testimonial injustice a vice. Bad effects are. Fricker contends that testimonial injustice produces moral and intellectual harms. Intellectually, it prevents the hearer from getting knowledge from the speaker. For instance, it prevents Greenleaf from getting knowledge from Marge, though Marge knows that Ripley killed Greenleaf's son. Morally, it degrades the speaker as a knower, and as a human.

This first key concept of vice corresponds exactly to the first key concept of virtue, explored in Chapter 2. But, do we really need to produce bad effects to be vicious? What if we just fail to produce good effects? If we fail to produce good effects, without producing bad effects, we are still missing out on goods. We are missing out on truths, and on opportunities to make the world better. According to this alternative concept of vice, any quality that fails to be a virtue constitutes a vice: a quality need not produce bad effects to be a vice; it need only *fail* to produce good effects. Here, the underlying intuition is that vices are defects, and one way to be defective is to fail to get external goods – to fall short.[4]

These two concepts are clearly in the same family. The difference between them is that the first key concept of vice treats virtues and vices as contraries; whereas the alternative above treats virtues and vices as contradictories. In other words, the first key concept allows for the possibility that we can simultaneously fail to have virtues and fail to have vices; whereas the alternative concept does not. To put the same point differently, only the first key concept allows for qualities that are neither virtues (because they do not produce good effects) nor vices (because they do not produce bad effects). To illustrate this point, consider the intellectual virtue that is featured on the television series *Lie to Me* (Fox, 2009–11), which dramatizes the work of psychologist Paul Ekman (2009). Characters in the series reliably detect when people are lying by observing their micro-facial expressions. Since this virtue is acquired, there are two ways to fail to have it. One might either: (a) be unreliable – one might produce more false than true beliefs about when people are lying based on their micro-expressions; or (b) be nonreliable – one might fail to produce any beliefs about when people are lying, based on their micro-expressions, by abstaining from learning the process. According to the first key concept of vice, only (a) is indicative of vice, because only (a) produces bad effects. But, according to the alternative concept, both (a) and (b) are indicative of vices because both miss out on valuable truths.

Is either one of these concepts of vice better, or worse, than the other? Whether we think so will likely depend on our philosophical intuitions. The problem is that our philosophical intuitions will differ in difficult cases. To illustrate: first, suppose I go through life without ever acquiring the virtue of detecting lies based on micro-expressions. As a result, I fail to form beliefs this way, and am sometimes ignorant of deception. Do I thereby have a vice? Some of us will think that I do, since I am missing out on some valuable truths. But, others will think that I do not, perhaps because these truths do not seem quite valuable enough. Second, do our intuitions change when we consider truths that *are* valuable enough? They may. Consider people who go through life without acquiring any of the virtues associated with critical thinking. Assume that the failure to acquire these virtues prevents such people from forming beliefs about a wide range of vital issues. The 2006 satirical film *Idiocracy* (Twentieth Century Fox, 2006) depicts a world like this, in which the future population of the earth suffers from widespread ignorance about a multitude of important issues, from the economy to human rights. Assume that such people are not producing false beliefs, but they are ignorant of truths. Are they vicious? Here, we may be more likely to opt for the alternative concept of vice. Finally, suppose you are in a world controlled by evil demons in which all of your beliefs turn out to be false. But, imagine that you manage to abstain from forming some specific type of beliefs about, say, what other people are thinking and feeling. Do you thereby have a vice? According to the first key concept of vice, abstaining is the ticket to avoiding vice in the demon-world. If you abstain, you are not forming false beliefs – you are not producing bad effects – and thus are not vicious. But, according to the alternative concept of vice, you do have a vice, since you are still missing out on valuable truths. Indeed, it seems that for the alternative concept, vice is unavoidable in the demon-world (Battaly 2014c).

   In short, the jury is still out on whether one of these concepts of vice is better, or worse, than the other. Each concept has its own advantages. The first key concept of vice allows children who have not yet acquired virtues to count among the nonvirtuous, instead of the vicious. The alternative concept of vice allows adults, like the people in *Idiocracy*, who are ignorant of a wide range of important truths to count among the vicious, rather than the nonvirtuous.

4.2 Motives Matter: Vices Require Bad Motives

Chapter 3 argued that producing good effects does not make a person virtuous, or is not the only thing that does. It also matters *why* one produces good effects. Analogously, one might contend that producing bad effects does not make a person vicious, or is not the only thing that does. It also matters *why* one produces bad effects. According to the second key concept of virtue and vice, motives are what matter: good motives are intrinsically good; bad motives are intrinsically bad. They are what ultimately make a person virtuous or vicious. Just as virtues get (some, or all, of) their positive value from good motives, vices will get (some, or all, of) their negative value from bad motives. In other words, according to the second key concept of vice, blameworthy psychological features, like bad motives, are *necessary* for vice. Producing bad effects is not enough.

But, why would bad motives be necessary for vice if one was already producing bad effects? Two guiding intuitions underlie this view. The first is that vices are blameworthy, and that we should only be blamed for things within our control. Arguably, we have greater control over our motives, which we acquire via practice, than we do over our effects in the world, which can be subject to luck. Suppose we have the bad luck of being in a world controlled by evil demons. In the demon-world, we produce bad effects – harm, false beliefs – but due to no fault of our own. Consequently, producing bad effects is not enough to make us vicious. Vice requires something for which we can be blamed. Arguably, we can be blamed for our motives; for example, we can be blamed for wanting to harm others, and for wanting to believe whatever is easiest. We can also be blamed for our dispositions to act, and for our conceptions of the good (our beliefs about what is good). Blameworthy features of our psychologies – for example, bad motives, dispositions to perform bad actions, and false conceptions of the good – are what is needed for vice. The second guiding intuition is that vices express character – they show us who we are as people. They reveal what we care about and value – they reveal our motives and our conceptions of the good. But, producing bad effects need not reveal what we care about or value. In the demon-world, we will produce bad effects even when our motives and values are exemplary. And animals and children can produce bad effects (false beliefs) in the absence of any acquired motives or values. In sum, one way for a person to be defective is to have a blameworthy psychology. Bad motives and false conceptions of the good make us worse people.

4.2.1 Aristotle on Vice

In *Nicomachean Ethics* VII, Aristotle endorses this second key concept of vice. He argues that to have a vice, one must have: (a) a disposition to perform acts that are in fact bad, (b) a false conception of the good, *and* (c) the motivation to perform said acts because one (falsely) believes that they are good. Aristotle thinks all of these features are blameworthy. He also thinks that (b) and (c) reveal what the vicious person cares about and values. In addition, he thinks the vicious person does not have any competing motivations – his motivations are thoroughly integrated with one another, and with his conception of the good. In other words, the vicious person is not conflicted. For Aristotle, the paradigms of vice include, for instance, self-indulgence, injustice, and cowardice. Following Aristotle, let's use the moral vice of self-indulgence as an illustration. We are all likely to be familiar with this vice. The self-indulgent person is obsessed with pleasure and anything that produces it. He consistently pursues and consumes objects that produce pleasure – food, drink, and sex – even when the objects are morally inappropriate. So, for instance, he (a) constantly watches all sorts of pornography (even the really bad sorts). Moreover, he is (c) motivated to do so because he (falsely) believes that pleasure is the most important good. His conception of the good is dominated by pleasure: he thinks that it is good to pursue pleasure above *all* else. But, according to Aristotle, he is objectively wrong: he overvalues pleasure, and is thus blind to other things of value. Consequently, (b) his conception of the good is false; and his actions and motives are objectively bad. Finally, we can stipulate that he is blameworthy for the above. He is not sick.

Hitler's vice of cruelty also uncontroversially meets all of Aristotle's conditions. Hitler (a) consistently performed acts that were in fact bad – he intentionally created policies that imprisoned, enslaved, and exterminated millions of people. He also falsely believed that his policies would make the world better. He and the Nazi leadership argued, in speeches and in writing, that the world should be "purified" of "inferior" races and repopulated by "the master race." Their "final solution" was to systematically exterminate the Jews in camps designed for that purpose. In other words, Hitler had (b) a horrifyingly false conception of the good. Finally, it appears that he and the Nazi leadership were (c) motivated to imprison, enslave, and exterminate Jews because they falsely believed that doing so was good. Hitler was blameworthy for all of this.[5] He also pursued his plan with conviction; he was neither conflicted, nor did he feel regret.

Let's now consider a controversial, but instructive, case. Does Cardinal Roger Mahoney, the former leader of the Catholic Church in Los Angeles, meet Aristotle's conditions for vice, specifically for the vice of injustice? For decades, Mahoney protected child-molesting clergy from prosecution by police. Beginning in the mid-1980s, Mahoney intentionally: relocated pedophile priests; advised them to avoid re-entering California until statutes of limitations on their acts of sexual abuse had expired; and encouraged them to avoid talking with therapists, who were mandatory reporters of abuse. In 2013, nearly 30 years after some of the abuse had taken place, the archdiocese of Los Angeles was compelled by a court order to turn over its records. Those records show that Mahoney (a) consistently privileged the rights of priests over the rights of victims. Arguably, these actions are paradigmatic of the vice of injustice. Mahoney also seemed to think that what he was doing was right. The *Los Angeles Times* reports that when asked (in 2010) by a victim's attorney whether it would have been right to contact the police, Mahoney replied that "today it would. But back then that isn't the way those matters were approached" (cited in Kim et al. 2013). Mahoney defends what he did, arguing that he was not a mandatory reporter of abuse, and that he was following church procedure – he sent priests to a specialized facility, itself run by clergy, for counseling. In his words, "we were never told that following these procedures was not effective . . . and that perpetrators were incapable of being treated [at the facility] [so] that they could safely pursue priestly ministry."[6] In short, Mahoney seems to have (b) false beliefs about which actions are right. Arguably, his actions were also (c) motivated by these false beliefs. So, Mahoney seems to meet Aristotle's conditions for vice.

But, determining whether a living person has a vice can be difficult. Mahoney's case is complicated for at least two reasons. First, Mahoney's actions in these matters are not entirely consistent. He reported a pedophile priest while serving as bishop in the early 1980s; and he has played a role in changing and improving the archdiocese's procedures for preventing child molestation. So, he may not fully satisfy Aristotle's condition (a). Second, Mahoney has apologized for his errors in handling the abuse, and has expressed concern for the victims. He appears to be conflicted, and to feel regret. So, his psychology may not be as fully integrated as that of a person with Aristotelian vice.

Relatedly, Aristotelian vice requires vicious agents to be blameworthy. And one might wonder whether Mahoney was blameworthy for his beliefs.[7] Mahoney believed that he was doing the right thing. He believed that it was right to send pedophile priests to a specialized facility for treatment rather than to report them. His beliefs were false – he wasn't doing the right thing. But, were his beliefs still justified? Was Mahoney blameless for having these beliefs? Now, it is true that *if* a person is blameless for his false beliefs, then he does not meet Aristotle's conditions for vice (Battaly 2014c). Suppose a person does everything he can to get true beliefs – he acquits himself admirably in searching for and considering a wide range of alternatives; he appropriately weighs all of the evidence; he has excellent reasons for holding the beliefs he holds; and so on. Nevertheless, his beliefs turn out to be false due to bad luck, and due to no fault of his own. This person is blameless for his false beliefs – it is not his fault that he ends up with false beliefs – so he doesn't meet Aristotle's conditions for vice. But, is Mahoney like this person? Is Mahoney similarly blameless for his beliefs? Arguably, he is not. Granted, psychological treatment of pedophilia has changed since the

1980s. Let's assume (for the sake of argument) that given the psychological knowledge at the time, Mahoney was justified in believing that the pedophile priests would benefit from the therapy they received. But, even if this is true, Mahoney still wasn't justified in believing that protecting them from prosecution was morally right. There are good moral arguments against harboring and protecting people who have committed violent crimes, even when those people are one's colleagues. Those moral arguments are inspired by a range of ethical views – including views as diverse as utilitarianism, Kantianism, and virtue ethics – and would have been readily available to Mahoney as an educated person living in a democracy. So, arguably, Mahoney was blameworthy for his beliefs – he should have known better. In sum, we have seen that Mahoney's case is complicated. We have some reasons to think that he satisfies Aristotle's conditions for vice, and some reasons to think that he does not.

Let's now consider an uncomplicated case of intellectual vice, one that clearly satisfies Aristotle's conditions: the vice of epistemic self-indulgence (Battaly 2010a). Epistemic self-indulgence is analogous in its structure to moral self-indulgence. Just as the morally self-indulgent person consistently consumes and enjoys food, drink, and sex that is in fact morally inappropriate, the epistemically self-indulgent person consistently consumes and enjoys propositions that are in fact epistemically inappropriate. Propositions can be true, or false, and can be about any topic, from Kate Middleton's hair color to the global economy. Some of these propositions are epistemically inappropriate, others are not. Clearly, falsehoods are epistemically inappropriate. What about truths – are some truths epistemically inappropriate? Could we be epistemically self-indulgent by consistently consuming truths? That depends on which truths we consistently consume, and on whether all truths are equally valuable. Arguably, some truths are more valuable than others; trivial truths about Middleton's hair color, or the number of threads in my left sock, are either not valuable at all, or not valuable enough. To lend support to this thesis, consider Mr. Casaubon, the character from George Eliot's *Middlemarch* (1984/1874). Arguably, Casaubon is epistemically self-indulgent because he consistently consumes and enjoys trivial truths. He spends his life compiling volumes of notes for a book he plans to write, but never does, *The Key to all Mythologies*. Of course, there are nontrivial truths about mythology, but the truths Casaubon consumes are not among them. He consumes "possible arguments . . . against his . . . view of the Philistine God dragon" (1984/1874: 191). While visiting Italy, he chooses to conduct research on "fish deities" rather than learn about Raphael's art. He is described as: "an elaborator of small explanations about as important as the surplus stock of false antiquities kept in a vendor's back chamber" (p. 199). Casaubon pursues his inquiries reflectively, and with conviction, thinking they are valuable. He has a conception of the epistemic good, in which his inquiries play the starring role. He even makes Dorothea edit his notes (pp. 457–458). Accordingly, Casaubon arguably satisfies Aristotle's conditions for vice. He (a) consistently consumes and enjoys propositions that are, in fact, epistemically inappropriate; he (b) has a false conception of the epistemic good; and he (c) is motivated to consume and enjoy such propositions because he falsely believes that they are epistemically good.

4.2.2   Alternatives to Aristotle's Analysis of Vice

Aristotle identifies one way in which blameworthy psychological features can make us vicious. In other words, his conditions are sufficient for vice.[8] They allow us to count dictators who falsely and negligently believe that they are doing good among the vicious. But, are all of his conditions necessary? Or, could we give different analyses of the second key concept of vice? There are two good reasons for thinking that some of Aristotle's conditions are not necessary.

The Villain. First, we might think that the sort of vice captured by Aristotle's analysis isn't insidious enough. After all, Aristotle's vicious people still want to do what they think is *good*! But, surely, ruthless villains who pursue what they think is bad are vicious. Since Aristotle's conditions (b) and (c) prevent such villains from counting among the vicious, we need an alternative analysis of vice. According to this alternative, the vicious person must have: (a) a disposition to perform acts that are in fact bad; (b') a true conception of the good and bad; and (c') the motivation to perform said acts because she (correctly) believes that they are bad. As above, all of these features are blameworthy; and (b') and (c') reveal what the vicious person cares about and values. As above, the vicious person's motives and beliefs must also be integrated. The vicious person acts with conviction, not regret.

The vice of cruelty also fits this alternative analysis. Michael Stocker (1979) and Robert Adams (2006) have both argued that we sometimes pursue the harm of others simply because we know it is bad, and want what is bad. We need not have an ulterior motive to get the good. In Adams's words: "People sometimes hate other people . . . and want bad things to happen to those they hate, not so that good things may come out of the bad, but just because they hate" (2006: 40). So, we can also conceive of a cruel dictator as one who (a) consistently harms others, and (b') knows that it is bad to harm others. This dictator (c') wants to harm others for precisely that reason. This analysis of cruelty captures just how bad cruelty can be. Jason Baehr (2010) has recently argued that there is an intellectual version of this vice of cruelty. Baehr calls it "epistemic malevolence." Roughly, a person is epistemically malevolent when he deliberately prevents others from getting knowledge, and does so because it is bad.[9]

The Slacker. Second, both of the above analyses of this concept of vice make vice difficult to get. To be vicious, a person must have a conception of what is good or bad. For Aristotle, she must have a (false) conception of the good. For the alternative above, she must have a (true) conception of the bad. In either case, she must have developed evaluative beliefs. But, isn't vice easier to get than this? What if we never bother to develop a conception of what is good or bad? Consider Roger Sterling, a character on the television series *Mad Men* (AMC, 2007–15) Sterling does exactly what a morally self-indulgent person would do – he consumes alcohol and sex excessively. But, he appears not to care about morality at all. In fact, the most disturbing feature of Sterling's character is his utter lack of any conception of the good or bad. Sterling doesn't perform actions because he thinks they are good, or bad; he just acts on his preferences, without bothering to evaluate them. Does this mean that he isn't vicious? This seems too easy a way out.

Instead, one might argue that Sterling still has the vice of moral self-indulgence. We are still vicious, when we fail to have a conception of the good or bad, provided that this failure is itself blameworthy. In Sterling's case, and the case of healthy adults, such failures are blameworthy. Sterling is clearly capable of asking questions about morality, and of evaluating his preferences. He just doesn't bother to do it. Consequently, his failure to develop a conception of the good or bad is blameworthy. According to this analysis, the vicious person must: (a) be disposed to perform acts that are in fact bad; while (~b) failing to have a conception of the good or bad; and (~c) failing to have motivations that are informed by any conception of value. The vicious person must also be blameworthy for (~b) and (~c). And she must not be con-flicted, or feel regret. Here, too, vice expresses who we are as people. Rather than revealing what we care about and value, it reveals that we haven't bothered to care or develop values. It expresses the *failure* to care about what is good or bad, and the *failure* to develop a conception of what is good or bad.

If the above is on the right track, then there is more than one good analysis of the second key concept of vice. Each of the three analyses above – Aristotle's, the Villain's, and the Slacker's – provide conditions that are sufficient for vice. But, each of the three also employs some conditions that are not necessary.

4.3 Weakness of Will and Vice

Can we fall short of virtue without having vice? Is it possible to fall somewhere in between the two? Recall Bill, who regu-larly cheats on Hilary. He knows it is bad to cheat, and wants to honor his commitment to Hilary, but simultaneously wants sex with other people. He continues to cheat, but feels terrible about it after the fact. Does Bill have a vice? Specifically, does he have the vice of moral self-indulgence?

Aristotle argues that people like Bill have weakness of will (*akrasia*), rather than vice. What does this mean? Compare Bill to Aristotle's morally self-indulgent person (see 4.2.1 above). Bill and the self-indulgent person will perform the same actions – for example, both will consistently cheat. But, their psychologies are different. In Aristotle's words: "*akrasia* is not vice . . . for *akrasia* is contrary to choice while vice is in accordance with choice" (NE.1151a6–7). For Aristotle, "choice" requires rational desire (*boulesis*). Roughly, one rationally desires x (e.g., pleasure) when one wants x (e.g., pleasure) because one believes it is good. The vicious person acts in accordance with her choice – in accordance with what she believes is good, though her beliefs are *false*. So, in having sex with others, the self-indulgent person does what she thinks is good: she (falsely) believes that pleasure is the most important good, and should always be pursued. She is not conflicted; she does not have competing motivations. She acts with conviction, not regret.

In contrast, the *akratic* person acts contrary to his choice – he acts contrary to what he believes is good; and his beliefs about the good are *true*. Bill correctly believes that honoring his commitment to Hilary is good, and cheating is bad. So, in having sex with others, Bill does something that he knows is bad. Bill is conflicted; he has competing motivations. On the one hand, he rationally desires honoring his commitment to Hilary. He wants to do right by her. But, on the other hand, he has an appetite for sex with other people. Aristotle thinks that appetites are desires, but not rational desires; they can compete with rational desires. Due to his appetites, Bill has sex with other people. Bill's actions are voluntary because he has options, and knows exactly what he is doing. So, he is blameworthy. Because he knows that having sex with others is bad, he feels regret.

In sum, on Aristotle's view, vice requires: (a) a disposition to perform acts that are in fact bad; (b) a false conception of the good; and (c) the motivation to perform said acts because one (falsely) believes that they are good. Whereas, weakness of will (*akrasia*) requires (a), while denying (b) and (c). Like the vicious person, the *akratic* person consistently performs bad acts. But, unlike the vicious person, the *akratic* person has a true conception of the good and bad, and is motivated to avoid performing those acts because he knows they are bad. He also has competing motivations – which bring about the bad acts – and feels awful about performing them.

Akrasia also occurs in the intellectual realm. Suppose that Sally, an experienced member of a scientific team, knows that she should stand up for her beliefs in the face of opposition from other team members (at least until there is sufficient evidence that she is wrong). She is motivated to stand up for her beliefs because she knows it is the right thing to do. She wants the team to get true beliefs, and she knows the team is more likely to get true beliefs if she sticks to her guns. Nevertheless, Sally consistently fails to stand up for her beliefs because she is simultaneously motivated to believe whatever will make her fit in. Because she acts contrary to her rational desires, she feels regret.

In a similar vein, consider the subjects in Solomon Asch's (1952) famous "conformity studies." In these studies, each subject is faced with unanimous opposition. That opposition is rigged – every group member, except the subject, is "in on" the experiment. Each group is presented with four lines, and asked: "Which two lines are the same length?" Every group member, except the subject, intentionally gives the same *obviously* false answer. Asch found that 33 percent of subjects subsequently gave the same false answer as the group. Like Sally, these subjects failed to stand up for their beliefs in the face of opposition – they yielded to group pressure. Asch explicitly argues that these subjects did not believe the group's opinion, and knew that they should have reported what they actually believed. Again, like Sally, these subjects reported feeling conflicted and guilty about "acting improperly" (1952: 472).

Virtue, vice, and *akrasia* are all qualities that reveal what we care about and value. Is Aristotle correct that *akrasia* falls somewhere between virtue and vice? According to the second key concept, virtues are praiseworthy, and vices are blameworthy. So, the answer seems to depend on whether the *akratic* person is too blameworthy to be virtuous, but also too praiseworthy to be vicious.

Recall from Chapter 3 that, for Aristotle, the virtuous person: consistently performs actions that are in fact good;

has a true conception of the good; and is motivated to perform said acts because she correctly believes that they are good. Aristotle also thinks that the virtuous person's motives and beliefs are thoroughly integrated; she is not conflicted. The *akratic* person is too blameworthy to be virtuous. After all, the *akratic* consistently performs acts that are in fact bad, and is blameworthy for doing so. The *akratic* is also blameworthy for developing the motivations that bring about those acts – Bill is blameworthy for wanting to have sex with others. But, like the virtuous person and unlike Aristotle's vicious person, the *akratic* is praiseworthy for developing a true conception of the good. He is also praiseworthy for wanting to do what he knows is good, and wanting to avoid what he knows is bad. Arguably, this makes him too praiseworthy to be vicious. To put the same point differently, consider the changes the *akratic* would have to make in order to become virtuous. Bill already has a true conception of the good and bad; and already wants to honor his commitment to Hilary because he knows that doing so is good. In other words, Bill has already done the hard work of developing values that are correct and rational desires that are correct. His appetites are the only stumbling block. If he could just train his appetites to be consistent with his rational desires, he would be virtuous. If he could change his appetite to have sex with others, then his rational desire to honor his commitment to Hilary would prevail, and his actions would follow suit. In short, unlike the self-indulgent person, Bill has already done much of the hard work that is required for virtue. He is much closer to getting the virtue of temperance than the self-indulgent person is.

It is worth noting that *akrasia* is also less blameworthy, and more praiseworthy, than the villain's vice and the slacker's vice. The villain and the *akratic* both perform bad actions. And both have true conceptions of the good and bad – both know what they are doing. But, the villain is blameworthy for wanting to perform those actions because they are bad; whereas, the *akratic* is praiseworthy for wanting to avoid those actions because they are bad, and for wanting to do what he knows is good. The slacker and the *akratic* also both perform bad actions. But, the slacker is blameworthy for failing to develop any conception of the good or bad; whereas, the *akratic* is praiseworthy for developing a true conception of the good and bad.

4.4   Self-Control and Virtue

Are there other ways to fall short of virtue without having vice? Suppose there is an election coming up, and you are in the process of forming beliefs about which candidates and policies are the best. You know that you are more likely to end up with true beliefs if you consider alternative points of view. And you do get yourself to consider alternatives. But, it is a struggle – you have to overcome the desire to ignore ideas that are different from your own. Do you fall short of virtue, specifically, the virtue of open-mindedness?

On the one hand, you know that you should consider alternatives, you are motivated to do so, and you consistently succeed in doing so – your actions are consistently good. You are also praiseworthy for all of this. Accordingly, you have much in common with the virtuous (open-minded) person. At the very least, you are neither vicious nor *akratic*, since you do not perform bad actions. But, on the other hand, you have competing motives, and have to work hard to do the right thing. Does a virtuous person have to work that hard; or is it relatively easy for her to do the right thing? Do you have the virtue of open-mindedness, or do you fall somewhere in between virtue and *akrasia*?

This is tricky, and hotly debated in the literature. For starters, Aristotle would claim that you aren't virtuous; instead, you are self-controlled (*enkratic*). He thinks that like the virtuous person, the self-controlled (*enkratic*) person: is disposed to perform actions that are in fact good; has a correct conception of the good; and is motivated to perform those actions because she correctly believes that they are good. But, unlike the virtuous person, the *enkratic* person also has "bad appetites" (NE.1152a1). The *enkratic* person is conflicted, whereas the virtuous person is not. The *enkratic* person has competing desires that make it difficult for her to do what she knows is right. In contrast, the motives, appetites and beliefs of the virtuous person are thoroughly integrated, making it easy for her to act. Accordingly, the virtuous person takes pleasure in performing acts that she knows to be right; whereas the *enkratic* person (who has to struggle to act well) does not.

Philippa Foot would also claim that you are *enkratic*, rather than virtuous. But, her view is slightly more nuanced than Aristotle's. In Foot's words:

> [W]e both are and are not inclined to think that the harder a man finds it to act virtuously the more virtue he shows if he does act well. For on the one hand great virtue is needed where it is particularly hard to act virtuously; yet on the other it could be argued that difficulty in acting virtuously shows that the agent is imperfect in virtue. (1997: 171)

Foot contends that there are two different kinds of things that make it hard for us to act well: bad luck in circumstances, and blameworthy flaws in character. On Foot's view, when our circumstances make it hard to act well, and we act well anyway, we demonstrate "great virtue." But, when flaws in character make it hard to act well, we are *enkratic* rather than virtuous. To illustrate, compare two people. Oksana lives in an oppressive society, in which information is strictly regulated, and internet access is limited to sites that endorse the views of the political party in power. Denise (like you) lives in a democratic society, in which information on all sorts of political views is widely available. Both Oksana and Denise struggle to consider alternative perspectives about political issues, and both consistently succeed in doing so. But, Oksana struggles because of her circumstances, whereas Denise struggles because she wants to ignore ideas that are different from her own. Oksana succeeds in considering alternatives despite the odds – she overcomes substantial societal obstacles. Arguably, she demonstrates great virtue in considering alternatives. In contrast, the obstacles Denise overcomes are of her own making – they are flaws in her character for which she is blameworthy. Denise still wants to ignore alternative ideas, even though she knows it is wrong to do so. Arguably, Denise's struggle demonstrates that she has not yet acquired virtue; instead she is *enkratic*.

Are Aristotle and Foot correct – should we endorse the distinction between virtue and *enkrateia*? On the one hand, they are correct that virtue is more praiseworthy than self-control. It is admirable to have eliminated desires that compete with one's correct conception of the good. But, on the other hand, Aristotle and Foot make virtue extremely difficult for ordinary human beings to acquire. After all, how many of us have eliminated all of our competing motivations? This raises an important issue. Should we treat virtue as an ideal, toward which ordinary human beings can make progress, but which few, if any, of us will ever achieve? Or, should we instead treat virtue as a state that is clearly within our reach – a state we can acquire if we work hard enough (and are lucky in our circumstances)?

Robert Roberts (1987) and Christine Swanton (2003) each make virtues slightly easier for human beings to acquire. Roberts argues that there are two different kinds of virtue: virtues of will power and motivational virtues. Motivational virtues – like generosity and justice – require an integrated psychology. But, virtues of will power – like self-control, patience, and courage – allow us to have competing motivations. Roberts thinks such qualities are virtues because they enable us to overcome those competing motivations (1987: 125). On his view, self-control (*enkrateia*) is a virtue because working hard to overcome competing motives and do the right thing is a praiseworthy achievement. So, unlike Aristotle and Foot, Roberts makes *some* virtues (virtues of will power) slightly easier for us to get.

Swanton makes all virtues slightly easier for us to acquire. She thinks that virtue is a "threshold concept" (2003: 24). She argues that since neither we nor our circumstances are perfect, our virtues need not be perfect either. They need only meet a threshold of being good enough. On her view, virtues are qualities of character that respond to the world in ways that are either excellent or good enough (2003: 19). Treating virtue as a threshold concept allows us to have competing motivations, and still have virtues. As long as our motivations are predominantly good, and we consistently do the right thing, a few stray competing motives won't prevent us from having virtue. We will still meet the threshold.[10] By relaxing the standard for virtue, Swanton makes it slightly easier for us to acquire virtues. Each of these views has advantages and disadvantages. If, like Aristotle and Foot, we maintain that virtue is an ideal state, then we can easily account for the intuition that the virtuous person does not have to struggle internally to do what is right. We can treat virtue as a goal, to which we can get progressively closer. We treat many important things in our lives this way – the ideal level of fitness, the ideal job, the ideal relationship – why should virtue be any different? But, we simultaneously risk making virtue too difficult to get, and we also risk making it difficult to use empirical psychology to learn about the virtues. (If few, or none, of us have virtues, then empirical psychology cannot generate measures for virtue.) On the other hand, if we relax the standard for virtue, then we make virtue slightly easier to acquire, and we make it more likely that we can use philosophy together with empirical psychology to learn about the virtues. Virtue will still be difficult to acquire, since it still requires meeting a threshold of predominantly good motives and good actions. So, we do not risk conflating virtue with *akrasia* or with vice. But, we do risk being unable to account for the intuition that the virtuous person acts with relative ease. We also risk eliminating the difference between virtue and self-control. Whether or not we ultimately decide to treat self-control as a virtue, at least one thing is clear. Self-control is neither vice nor *akrasia*. At best, self-control (*enkrateia*) is a virtue; at worst, it falls between virtue and *akrasia*.

5
Virtue, Right Action, and Knowledge

Why should we care about virtues like benevolence and open-mindedness? If the views in Chapter 3 deliver on their promissory note, then we will have at least one reason to care about these virtues: they are intrinsically valuable. Do we have additional reasons to care about them? For instance, does having these virtues mean that we will always do the right thing, or always get knowledge? In other words, are these virtues *sufficient* for performing right acts, or getting knowledge? In addition, are these virtues *necessary* for right action, or knowledge – could we perform right acts, or get knowledge, without them? Some philosophers think that the virtues are connected to right action, and knowledge, in exactly these ways. They argue that the virtues, or, more specifically, components of the virtues, are necessary and sufficient for right action, or knowledge. Accordingly, Rosalind Hursthouse has argued that components of the moral virtues are both necessary and sufficient for performing right acts (1997: 219), while Linda Zagzebski (1996: 271) has argued that components of the intellectual virtues are both necessary and sufficient for knowledge.[1] If Hursthouse and Zagzebski are correct, then we have additional reasons to care about the virtues. After all, if they are correct, we can't perform right acts or get knowledge without the virtues, or components thereof.

Are Hursthouse and Zagzebski correct? This chapter suggests that they are not. It even suggests that there may not be any necessary and sufficient connections between components of the virtues on the one hand, and right action, or knowledge, on the other. But, necessary and sufficient connections are not the only game in town; nor, for our purposes, are they the most important. More important are probabilistic connections between the virtues and our real-life attempts to perform right acts and get knowledge. In the real world, we *often* need to do what a virtuous person would do in order to perform a right act or get knowledge, even if we don't *always* need to do so. And, in the real world, doing what a virtuous person would do *often* results in a right act, or produces knowledge, even if it doesn't *always* do so. This means that even if components of the virtues are neither strictly necessary nor sufficient for right acts or knowledge, looser connections still hold. Accordingly, we still have additional reasons to try to be virtuous and to care about virtues. Since we care about performing right acts and getting knowledge in the real world, we should also care about developing the components of the virtues that help us do so.

5.1 Components of the Virtues

This chapter focuses on the second key concept of virtue, according to which virtues are acquired, praiseworthy dispositions of action and motivation. Recapping Chapter 3, to have the moral virtue of benevolence, one must consistently perform a particular kind of action – one must help others appropriately. And one must do so because of one's motivations – one must consistently care about the good, and about the well-being of others. Recall that philosophers disagree about whether virtues like benevolence require consistent success in producing external goods (e.g., actually improving the well-being of others). Likewise, to have the intellectual virtue of open-mindedness, one must consistently consider alternative ideas appropriately. And, one must do so because one consistently cares about truth, and about considering alternatives. Philosophers also disagree about whether virtues like open-mindedness require consistent success in getting the truth. In Chapter 4, we saw that Aristotle's version of the second key concept of virtue also requires an integrated psychology – if we have competing motivations, then we don't have virtues. Whether or not virtues like benevolence and open-mindedness require success in producing external goods, and whether or not they require integrated psychologies, one thing is abundantly clear. Such virtues will be difficult to acquire. We are not born with the dispositions of action and motivation that are needed for virtue. The disposition to help others appropriately is not innate; we need to *learn* who to help, how to help, and when to help. Nor are we born with the disposition to care appropriately about truth; we need to *learn* to care more about truth than we care about believing what will make us feel good. Acquiring the appropriate dispositions will, at minimum, involve repeated practice, appropriate guidance, an appropriate environment, and luck in genetics. It will not be easy. At maximum, it will be practically impossible for most humans to possess virtues.

This means that if we need to fully possess virtues in order to perform right acts, or get knowledge, then we aren't likely to perform *any* right acts or have *any* knowledge! In other words, requiring *full virtue possession* for right action, or knowledge, is likely to land us in skepticism. Nor does full virtue possession automatically entail that we always perform right acts, or get knowledge. If we fully possess the moral virtues, then we *consistently* act in ways that are characteristic of those virtues; and if we fully possess Zagzebski-style intellectual virtues, then we *reliably* get true beliefs. But, consistency and reliability are fallible. Even fully virtuous people occasionally have bad days – they get sick or exhausted. And when they do, they act in uncharacteristic ways and produce beliefs that are false. For these reasons, neither Hursthouse nor Zagzebski ties full virtue possession to right action or knowledge. Both recognize that it is much easier to have knowledge, and to perform right acts, than it is to fully possess virtues. Instead, each ties right action and knowledge to *components of virtue*, which are easier to get, and which we can get without fully possessing virtue.

One such component is performing a *virtuous act*. To perform a virtuous act, I need only do what a virtuous person *would* characteristically do *if* she were in my situation. A virtuous (benevolent, or open-minded, etc.) person is one who fully possesses the virtue (benevolence, or open-mindedness, etc.) in question. A virtuous person need not actually be in my situation, for me to perform a virtuous act. To perform a virtuous act, my act need only match what she *would* characteristically do *if* she were in my situation. Suppose I see a student drop a pile of books. If, in this situation, a virtuous person would help pick up the books, then helping to pick up the books is a virtuous act.

There are six key points to make about a virtuous act. First, one can perform a virtuous act on a single occasion. One can do what a virtuous person would do on one occasion, even if one doesn't *consistently* do what a virtuous person would do. A virtuous act can be a "one-off." For instance, in volunteering at a homeless shelter on a single afternoon, I perform a virtuous act, even if I never volunteer at a homeless shelter again. I don't need to consistently volunteer at the homeless shelter in order to perform a virtuous act. Second, one can perform a virtuous act even if one does not have the same motives as a virtuous person. I can volunteer at the homeless shelter, not because I care about people who are homeless, but because I care about puffing up my college applications. Third, consequently, one can perform a virtuous act without fully possessing the virtue in question. I can volunteer at a homeless shelter on a single occasion, and thus perform a virtuous act, even though I lack the virtue of benevolence. That virtue requires consistently helping others appropriately, and consistently caring about others. This means that, fourth, virtuous acts are not the same as acts that issue from virtues, however odd this may sound. Granted, in virtuous people, virtuous acts do issue from virtues. But, the rest of us can perform virtuous acts without possessing the virtues. Fifth, this also means that it is much easier to perform a virtuous act than it is to possess a virtue. But, finally, not every case of matching what a virtuous person would characteristically do counts as a virtuous act. If we do what a virtuous person would characteristically do either involuntarily or by accident, then we do not perform a virtuous act.

What is the upshot of this technical definition of a *virtuous act*? Virtuous acts are simply acts that a virtuous person would characteristically perform if she were in the same situation. Though it may sound strange, people who do not possess virtues can perform virtuous acts.

5.2   Are Components of Moral Virtue Necessary and Sufficient for Right Action?

One standard objection to virtue ethics is that, unlike Kantian ethics and utilitarianism, virtue ethics does not guide our conduct – it does not tell us what we should do. One of the functions of an ethical theory is to help us figure out what we should do in real-life situations. So, it is indeed a problem if virtue ethics can't do this. Kantian ethics and utilitarianism try to guide our conduct by offering accounts of right action. Accordingly, in replying to the objection, Rosalind Hursthouse also offers an account of right action. In "Virtue Theory and Abortion," she argues that right acts are virtuous acts (as defined above). In her words: "An action is right [if and only if] it is what a virtuous agent would do in the circumstances" (1997: 219).[2] So, one should do whatever a virtuous person would do in the same situation. Now, you might wonder whether this advice is simply vacuous. Suppose a friend is considering an abortion. How helpful would it be to advise her to "do what a virtuous person would do"?

Hursthouse argues that the directive to do what a virtuous person would do is far from vacuous. On the contrary, it provides us with guidance, while recognizing that it is sometimes difficult to know what we should do. To explicate, Hursthouse thinks that each virtue and vice generates its own rule – for example, do what is kind, humble, or generous; do not do what is callous, arrogant, or greedy (1999: 37). She argues that in choosing abortion, a girl who is genuinely and wholly unprepared for motherhood may well be doing what is humble, and thus what is right. Whereas, a woman who chooses abortion so that she can continue to "have a good time" may well be doing what is greedy, and thus not right

(1997: 234). Hursthouse acknowledges that it is sometimes difficult to apply rules like "do what is humble" and "do not do what is greedy." But she thinks this is as it should be. After all, it is sometimes difficult to know what we should do in real life, for example, with respect to abortion. She argues that an ethical theory should reflect this difficulty; it should not spit out easy answers about what we should do in difficult cases. If a theory does spit out easy answers, then this indicates that it has failed to capture the complexity and nuance of action in the real world.

Is Hursthouse's account of right action correct? For starters, let's remind ourselves that Hursthouse is *not* arguing that full virtue possession is necessary and sufficient for performing a right act. We can do the right thing without fully possessing any moral virtues. Cardinal Mahoney is far from fully possessing the virtue of justice, and may even possess the vice of injustice (see Chapter 4 above). But, on the rare occasion when he did report a pedophile priest, he clearly did the right thing. Full virtue possession is not necessary for right action. Nor is it sufficient. Suppose Alice Paul does fully possess the virtue of courage (see Chapter 1 above). She might still have occasionally failed to do the right thing. Perhaps she occasionally broke a promise to give a speech due to her dread of public speaking. Hursthouse agrees with all of this. She is instead arguing that *virtuous acts* are necessary and sufficient for right acts. Is this correct?

In *On Virtue Ethics*, Hursthouse refines her account of right action. She recognizes that even virtuous people occasionally have bad days – they occasionally act in ways that are uncharacteristic of the virtues they possess. For instance, we can assume that Alice Paul occasionally failed to act in ways that were characteristic of the virtue of courage. Accordingly, Hursthouse revises her account as follows: "An action is right [if and only if] it is what a virtuous agent would *characteristically* (i.e., acting in character) do in the circumstances" (1999: 28; my emphasis). So, even if Paul occasionally broke a promise to speak, such acts are not characteristic of the virtue of courage, and thus are not part of Hursthouse's account of right action. Of course, this is a very minor revision to her view; one that we have already accounted for in the definition of virtuous acts above.

So, are virtuous acts sufficient for right acts? In other words, is it true that whenever we do what a virtuous person would characteristically do, we perform a right act? Can you think of any examples where this is false – where we do what a virtuous person would characteristically do, but do not perform a right act? Suppose that Arif is a civilian who lives in a country in which a revolution has just now begun. With no forewarning, soldiers detain everyone in Arif's building (all civilians) including Arif. All 40 are held at gunpoint. The soldiers single out Arif and one other detainee. They give Arif a gun and tell him that if he doesn't kill the other detainee, then they will kill the remaining 38. If he does kill the other detainee, then all of the remaining detainees will be set free. Either way, Arif will be set free. Everything the soldiers say is true; and there is no way for Arif to get out of this situation. If, for instance, he tries to kill himself, or tries to escape, or kill the soldiers, then they will kill all the detainees, including Arif. Nor can Arif be blamed for being in this situation – there is no way that he could have predicted the revolution. He is, as we sometimes say, "just in the wrong place at the wrong time."

What would a virtuous person characteristically do, if she were in this situation? And would her action be right? It is hard to say what a virtuous person would do in this situation. Since the consequences would be worse if she refused to kill the detainee, she may kill the detainee. But, she may instead opt to allow the other detainees to be killed, rather than actively kill any detainee herself. Interestingly, we need not determine what a virtuous person would characteristically do in this situation in order to determine that her action would not be right. This is because no matter what she does, her action would not be right. This situation is one in which none of the actions open to the agent is right. Philosophers refer to situations like this as "tragic dilemmas" and "dirty hands cases": no matter what the agent does, she cannot emerge without dirty hands. In Hursthouse's words, a virtuous agent emerges from a tragic dilemma "having done a terrible thing, the very sort of thing . . . [a] vicious agent would characteristically do – killed someone, or let them die, betrayed a trust, violated someone's . . . rights" (1999: 74).

Surprisingly, Hursthouse herself acknowledges that none of the actions open to a virtuous agent in a tragic dilemma – for example, killing the detainee, allowing others to die, etc. – would be right. She argues that right actions are "good deeds" that "merit praise rather than blame . . . act[s] that an agent can take pride in doing rather than feeling unhappy about" (1999: 46). And she recognizes that none of the actions above merits approval; none is an act that the agent should feel happy about. In other words, Hursthouse herself acknowledges that virtuous acts are *not sufficient* for right acts. In tragic dilemmas, it is impossible to perform a right act. So, in tragic dilemmas, even if we do what a virtuous person would characteristically do, we do not perform a right act. Accordingly, Hursthouse revises her view: "An action is right [if and only if] it is what a virtuous agent would characteristically do, *except for tragic dilemmas*" (1999: 79; my emphasis).[3]

So, virtuous acts do not *always* result in right acts. But, virtuous acts still *often* result in right acts. This is because most of the moral situations we encounter in the real world are not tragic dilemmas.[4] Thankfully, tragic dilemmas are relatively rare (in much of the developed world). *Most* of the time, when we do what a virtuous person would characteristically do, we do what is right. To illustrate, suppose you are a graduating senior, who is looking for a job. If you can't find a job, you will still be able to live with your roommates. Though jobs are somewhat scarce, you manage to land an interview for a highly paid position at a terrific company. The interviewer explains that the person who gets the job must already have work experience in the field. She asks whether you do. As a matter of fact, you do not, not even close. Provided that you must answer, you can either lie or tell the truth. If you lie, and aren't found out, you will get the job. What would a virtuous person characteristically do in this situation? The answer is easy: a virtuous person, specifically an honest person, would tell the truth. In this situation, it is also clearly right to tell the truth. It is clearly right even if we think it is right for some other reason – for example, because telling the truth treats the interviewer as an end in herself, or because a policy of truth-telling will produce the best consequences overall. (We return to this idea below.) The point is that in this situation, and the many others like it, doing what a virtuous person would do results in performing a right act. In short, even though virtuous acts are *not sufficient* for right acts, virtuous acts are still *usually* right.

Are virtuous acts necessary for right acts? In other words, must we perform a virtuous act in order to perform a right act? Can you think of any cases where this is false – where we perform right acts, but don't do what a virtuous person would characteristically do? Imagine it is midnight, and your *Procrastinating Roommate* has a 10-page paper due in his 8:00 a.m. class. He has not yet started the paper, despite the fact that he has known about it for months. Unfortunately, this is typical of him; he is on the verge of failing out of college. He can't get an extension, and not handing something in will result in his failing out. He has a decision to make: download someone else's paper, or hand in nothing and fail out of college, or genuinely resolve to change his ways starting now. Suppose he genuinely resolves to change his ways. Accordingly, he writes until dawn, and hands in a paper, though not a great paper. Notice that the Procrastinating Roommate performs actions that a virtuous person would not characteristically perform. After all, a virtuous person, specifically a diligent person, would not have procrastinated in the first place. She would not be in this situation. Nor would she need to improve her character. In short, the Procrastinating Roommate does not do what a virtuous person would characteristically do. But, the Procrastinating Roommate still performs right acts. He merits praise and approval for resolving to change his ways; he does a good deed, in which he can take pride, etc. Accordingly, virtuous acts are *not necessary* for right acts.

Robert Johnson defends this point in "Virtue and Right" (2003). Johnson asks us to imagine a *Chronic Liar* who has decided to reform his character. In an effort to stop lying, he keeps track of his lies and of his progress in telling the truth. When tempted to lie, he reminds himself that people often don't have negative responses to the truth, and so on. (Imagine a 12-step program for liars.) Johnson argues that a virtuous person would not perform any of these acts. Unlike the Chronic Liar, a virtuous person, specifically an honest person, wouldn't lie to begin with. Nor would she need to make up for past wrongdoing, or need to reform her character. And, yet, the actions of the Chronic Liar are still right. In Johnson's words, such acts are "truly excellent" (2003: 825). In short, the Chronic Liar performs right acts without performing virtuous acts. More generally, in *developing* virtues, we sometimes perform right acts without performing virtuous acts. So, to reiterate, this shows that virtuous acts are *not necessary* for right acts.

Hursthouse has not addressed counter-examples like the Procrastinating Roommate and the Chronic Liar, in which the agent is reforming his character. But, she does address examples that involve past wrongdoing. In those examples she bites the bullet: she continues to maintain that virtuous acts *are necessary* for right acts. To illustrate, she considers a *Player* who has "sweet-talked" two different women, A and B, into getting pregnant by promising to marry each of them. He can only marry one. Note that a virtuous person would never be in this situation in the first place. Suppose that B has found ample independent means of supporting herself. Accordingly, Hursthouse argues, it would be worse for the Player to break his promise to A than to break his promise to B. Hence, the right *decision* is for him to marry A. But, Hursthouse claims that in marrying A and breaking his promise to B, the Player still does not perform a right *act*. In her words, this is because "he merits not praise, but blame, for having created the circumstances that made it necessary for him to abandon B" (1999: 47). In short, Hursthouse argues that his act is not praiseworthy, and thus not right. Moreover, she thinks this is precisely the answer we should expect. After all, the Player cannot do what a virtuous person would characteristically do in this situation, since a virtuous person would never be in this situation. And, since performing a right act requires doing what a virtuous person would characteristically do, the Player cannot perform a right act.

Is there anything suspicious about Hursthouse's example or her argument? For starters, her example entails that there are some acts we *should* do, even though they are not *right*.[5] The Player *should* marry A, even though marrying A is not *right*.[6] It is not *right* because it is not praiseworthy; but it is nevertheless what he *should* do – given the circumstances, the other options (marrying B, or marrying neither A nor B) would be callous, and thus wrong. In short, Hursthouse thinks that some of the acts that we *should* perform are not *right*. You may find this suspicious; Kantians and utilitarians do. They argue that right acts just are the acts that we should perform, and vice versa. Accordingly, you may think that the Player does perform a right act, at least in the sense that he does what he should do. Second, you may even think that the Player performs a right act, in the sense that he does something excellent and praiseworthy. Perhaps, there is something praiseworthy in marrying A; perhaps he does a good deed. But, even if the Player doesn't perform a right act in the latter sense, the Procrastinating Roommate and the Chronic Liar still do. (They also perform right acts in the sense of doing what they should do.) Hence, *contra* Hursthouse, we can still conclude that virtuous acts are *not necessary* for right acts.

This means that we don't *always* need to do what a virtuous person would do in order to perform a right act. Virtuous acts are not strictly necessary for right acts. Nevertheless, we still *often* need to do what a virtuous person would do in order to perform a right act. This is because we often find ourselves in real-world situations that a virtuous person would also be in! The three examples above show that we *sometimes* create situations that a virtuous person would never be in. But, we shouldn't lose the forest for the trees. In developing the virtues, we encounter a *plethora* of situations that a virtuous person would be in. And, in those situations, we won't perform right acts unless we do what a virtuous person would do. To illustrate, recall the *Job Interview* example. The interviewer asks whether you have work experience in the field. You do not. Assume that you must answer, and that you can either lie or tell the truth. First, this is clearly a situation that we (who are developing virtues) can share with virtuous people. Second, in this situation, it is wrong to lie and right to tell the truth. It is right even if we think it is right for a Kantian or utilitarian reason (see below). Third, it is clear that telling the truth is what a virtuous person would do in this situation.[7] It follows that if we didn't do what a virtuous person would do in this situation – namely, tell the truth – then we wouldn't perform a right act.[8] So, the point is that in this situation, and the many others like it, doing what a virtuous person would do is needed for performing a right act. In sum, even though virtuous acts are *not always* needed for right acts, virtuous acts are still *often* needed for right acts.

To sum up the discussion thus far, the connections between virtuous acts and right acts are probabilistic. Virtuous acts are often needed for right acts, and usually result in right acts. But, they are neither strictly necessary nor strictly sufficient for right acts. There is one final wrinkle. In the Job Interview example, doing what a virtuous person would do (telling the truth) results in performing a right act, and is needed to perform a right act. But, the fact that a virtuous person would tell the truth in this situation may not be what *makes* the act right. Telling the truth may be right not *because* it is what a virtuous person would do, but *because* it treats the interviewer as an end in herself, or because it produces the best consequences overall. Similarly, donating money to a hospital may be right because it reduces suffering, not because it is what a virtuous person would do. Keeping a promise to a friend may be right because it respects her as a person, not because it is what a virtuous person would do.[9]

We have seen that virtuous acts and right acts are probabilistically connected. This is true even if virtuous acts don't ultimately explain rightness; even if we give a Kantian or utilitarian explanation of rightness.[10] This means that the acts of virtuous people are reliable guides to right action – virtuous acts track right acts – whatever our view of rightness. In other words, we can reliably figure out which acts are right by figuring out what a virtuous person would do, even if a virtuous person's performing such acts doesn't make them right. Analogously, the readings of a good thermometer are a reliable guide to temperature: we can reliably figure out the temperature by consulting a good thermometer, even though the readings of a good thermometer do not make the temperature what it is. To come full circle, virtue ethics can provide us with useful guidance about what to do. We have learned that what a virtuous person would do is usually right. So, given that we can often figure out what a virtuous person would do, we can figure out which acts are likely to be right.

5.3 Are Components of Intellectual Virtue Necessary and Sufficient for Knowledge?

Are components of intellectual virtue necessary and sufficient for knowledge? Linda Zagzebski thinks they are.[11] On her view: "Knowledge is a state of true belief arising out of acts of intellectual virtue" (1996: 271). In other words, a person knows that p (for any proposition) if and only if: she believes that p, p is true, and her belief results from an act of intellectual virtue. For instance, Einstein knows that $E = mc^2$ if and only if: he believes that $E = mc^2$, $E = mc^2$ is true, and his belief that $E = mc^2$ is the result of an act of intellectual virtue. Nearly all analyses of knowledge include a belief condition (knowledge is a mental state), a truth condition (knowledge can't be false), and a third condition that is supposed to prevent the belief from turning out to be true by accident (lucky guesses aren't knowledge). Zagzebski's unique contribution is to argue that the third condition is a component of intellectual virtue, specifically, an act of intellectual virtue.

What is an *act of intellectual virtue*? According to Zagzebski:

> [An act of intellectual virtue is] an act that arises from the motivational component of [the virtue in question], is something a person with [the] virtue would . . . do in the circumstances, is successful in achieving the end of the . . . motivation, and is such that the agent acquires a true belief . . . through these features of the act. (1996: 270)

Let's unpack this definition. We'll use the virtue of open-mindedness to illustrate it, but we could use any intellectual virtue (intellectual autonomy, intellectual courage, etc.). To perform an act of open-mindedness, four conditions must be met. First, one must have the same motivations that an open-minded person would have. This means that one must consistently be motivated to: (a) get truth, and (b) consider alternative perspectives. In short, one must share the motivations of the open-minded person. Second, one must, on this occasion, succeed in attaining the end of one's motivation to

(b) consider alternative perspectives. Put more simply, one must, on this occasion, do what an open-minded person would do, if she were in the same situation. In other words, one must perform an open-minded act. This should sound familiar from our discussion above. Here, Zagzebski is merely applying the concept of a virtuous act to the intellectual realm. Third, one must, on this occasion, succeed in attaining the end of one's motivation to (a) get truth. This means that one must, on this occasion, get a true belief. Finally, fourth, one must get a true belief on this occasion because of one's action and motivation. The goal of the fourth condition is to rule out cases in which one gets a true belief because of luck.[12]

There are two important points to make about an act of intellectual virtue. First, odd though this may sound, an *act of intellectual virtue* is not identical to an *intellectually virtuous act*. To illustrate: an act of open-mindedness is not identical to an open-minded act. We perform an open-minded act whenever we do what an open-minded person would characteristically do in the same situation. Performing an open-minded act is the second condition above. This means that to perform an *act of* open-mindedness, we must perform an open-minded act, but we must also do much more. To perform an *act of* open-mindedness, we must also have the same motivations as the open-minded person, get the truth, and get it because of our actions and motivations. To put the same point differently, whenever we perform an act of open-mindedness, we thereby perform an open-minded act. But, it is not true that whenever we perform an open-minded act, we thereby perform an act of open-mindedness. Second, on Zagzebski's view, we can perform an act of intellectual virtue without fully possessing the intellectual virtue in question. Recall that for Zagzebski, the virtue of open-mindedness is a disposition of motivation and success. To fully possess the virtue of open-mindedness, we must consistently be motivated to: (a) get truth and (b) consider alternative perspectives. But, we must also consistently succeed in: (a) getting true beliefs and (b) considering perspectives that we should. Performing an act of open-mindedness does require that we share the motivations of the open-minded person. But, it does not require that we *consistently* consider perspectives that we should, or consistently get true beliefs (as a result). It only requires that we do what an open-minded person would do, and thereby get a true belief, on this *one occasion*. Accordingly, I might perform acts of open-mindedness from time to time, even though I haven't yet acquired a settled habit of doing what an open-minded person would do. In short, one can perform an act of open-mindedness without fully possessing the virtue of open-mindedness. One can also fully possess the virtue of open-mindedness, but *occasionally* fail to perform acts of open-mindedness. Even virtuous people sometimes have bad days.[13]

So, is Zagzebski correct? Are acts of intellectual virtue necessary and sufficient for knowledge? For starters, let's consider whether there is more than one kind of knowledge. Arguably, there is one kind of knowledge that requires active inquiry and effort on our part (high-grade knowledge), and another kind of knowledge that we can acquire passively and involuntarily (low-grade knowledge). To illustrate the difference, first suppose that you are a police detective investigating a murder. There are no witnesses. In order to know who committed the murder, you must conduct an inquiry: you must form a hypothesis, search for confirming and disconfirming evidence, consider alternative suspects, etc. In short, you must actively do something in order to get this kind of knowledge. In contrast, suppose that you are sitting in a well-lighted room that is painted white. You don't need to conduct an inquiry in order to know that the walls are white. Arguably, you can know the color of the walls without doing much of anything. Given that your eyes are open, and your eyes and brain are functioning properly, you will automatically know that they are white. Perceptual knowledge of our surroundings seems to be low-grade, whereas much scientific, economic, medical, and evaluative knowledge seems to be high-grade. High-grade knowledge need not be about theoretical academic subjects: you can have high-grade knowledge about which apartment will be best to rent, or about which Major will best suit your interests.

Suppose, for the moment, that the distinction between low-grade and high-grade knowledge is legitimate. If so, low-grade knowledge isn't the kind of knowledge that will require acts of intellectual virtue. After all, to perform an act of intellectual virtue, you must do what an intellectually virtuous person would do in the same situation – for example, consider alternatives, search for evidence, etc. But, you can know that the wall is white without doing anything of the sort. You don't need to consider alternatives, or search for evidence. Given that your eyes are open, your belief that the wall is white is automatic and involuntary; and will (arguably) count as knowledge, provided that it is the result of Sosa-style intellectual virtues.[14] So, let's set low-grade knowledge aside, and see whether Zagzebski is correct about high-grade knowledge.

Are acts of intellectual virtue sufficient for high-grade knowledge? In other words, is it true that whenever we perform an act of intellectual virtue, we get high-grade knowledge? Can you think of any examples where this is false – where we perform an act of intellectual virtue, but do not get high-grade knowledge? Finding sufficient conditions for knowledge (of any kind) has been a notorious problem in contemporary epistemology. Here is the back-story. In the mid-twentieth century, most epistemologists thought that a person had knowledge if and only if he had a (1) true (2) belief that was (3) backed by good reasons or evidence. The third condition – having good reasons or evidence – was supposed to prevent the person from ending up with a true belief by accident. Epistemologists (in every time period) agree that when we end up with true beliefs because of luck, we do not have knowledge. Enter Edmund Gettier. In 1963, Gettier published a devastating two-page paper which showed that the conditions above are not sufficient for knowledge. In other words, he argued that we sometimes meet these conditions, but lack knowledge. We lack knowledge because we still end up with true beliefs because of luck. The third condition does not do the job it is supposed to do. To illustrate Gettier's point, suppose you believe that "Austin owns a Mac." You have excellent evidence for this belief: you have seen Austin with a Mac on multiple occasions, and he has repeatedly told you that he owns a Mac. Now, suppose you validly deduce (via existential introduction) the further belief that "Someone in Austin's Intro to Philosophy class owns a Mac."[15] Since you have excellent evidence for your first belief (Austin owns a Mac), you also have excellent evidence for your second belief (Someone in Austin's Intro to Philosophy class owns a Mac). Focus on the second belief. Shockingly, it turns out that Austin does *not* own a Mac – he was participating in an elaborate ruse. That is the first twist. Here comes the second twist. Someone else in his Intro to Philosophy class *does* own a Mac. Accordingly, your belief that "Someone in Austin's Intro to Philosophy class owns a Mac" is backed by excellent evidence, and ends up being true. But, it ends up being true because of luck. Hence, it is not knowledge. You have met the three conditions above, but you still don't know that "Someone in Austin's Intro to Philosophy class owns a Mac." In sum, Gettier shows that we can have good evidence, but still arrive at true beliefs because of luck. This means that true beliefs that are backed by good evidence are not sufficient for knowledge. Since 1963, epistemologists have proposed multiple different third conditions, in an attempt to solve the Gettier problem. Thus far, none of those conditions has succeeded.

Has Zagzebski found a way to solve the Gettier problem? Are acts of intellectual virtue sufficient for knowledge? Recall that Zagzebski intends the fourth condition of an act of intellectual virtue to rule out cases in which we get true beliefs because of luck. Does her account succeed? Or, are acts of intellectual virtue (like every other proposed solution before them) still ultimately subject to the Gettier problem? Arguably, they are still subject to the Gettier problem. Suppose that Brenda, a police detective, is investigating the murder of an accountant who worked for a multibillion dollar corporation.[16] Nobody witnessed the murder. Brenda cares about getting the truth, cares about considering alternative suspects, and cares about searching for and evaluating evidence. In short, she shares the motivations of the intellectually virtuous person. For the sake of simplicity, let's suppose that there are only two suspects: the CEO of the corporation, and the victim's husband. The evidence reveals that the husband despised his wife. It also reveals that the accountant concealed the corporation's income, that the government was conducting an investigation of the corporation, and that the CEO's fingerprints were on the murder weapon. Suppose that most of the evidence points toward the CEO, and that Brenda is thus inclined to believe that the CEO committed the murder. But, because she is motivated to get the truth and cares about considering alternative scenarios, she asks her team of detectives for their views. In seeking their views, she does what an intellectually virtuous person would do. Here is the first twist. Unbeknownst to Brenda or her team, the corporation, in an effort to protect its own interests, has brainwashed her team into believing that the husband committed the murder. So, when Brenda asks her team for their views, they confidently and unanimously claim that the husband did it, and that she has misinterpreted the evidence. In evaluating the options, Brenda, "out of an earnest openness to [her] colleagues' views and a keen awareness of [her] own fallibility," comes to believe that the husband did it (Baehr 2006: 488). Here is the second twist. Benda's belief turns out to be correct; the husband is, indeed, the murderer. It is important to point out that Brenda arrived at her true belief about the identity of the murderer because of her intellectually virtuous actions and motivations: if she hadn't done the same thing that a virtuous person would do – if she hadn't included the views of her colleagues in her deliberations – then she wouldn't have arrived at a true belief. So, Brenda seems to satisfy all four conditions of an act of intellectual virtue. But, she still doesn't know that the husband did it! She doesn't know because luck has still managed to creep in – the fourth condition hasn't ruled it out. It was just lucky that the belief that the corporation inculcated in her team happened to be true. If the above is correct, then acts of intellectual virtue are still subject to the Gettier problem; and, thus, acts of intellectual virtue are *not sufficient* for high-grade knowledge.

But, is the above correct? On behalf of Zagzebski, one might reply that the example above doesn't really satisfy the fourth condition of an act of intellectual virtue – that Brenda doesn't really arrive at a *true* belief, rather than a false one, because of her intellectually virtuous actions and motivations. Granted, Brenda's intellectually virtuous actions and motivations are causally involved in getting a true belief about the identity of the murderer – it is a fact that if she hadn't performed those actions and had those motivations, then she wouldn't have arrived at a true belief. But, she doesn't get a true belief, rather than a false one, primarily because of her intellectually virtuous actions and motivations; instead, she gets a *true* belief primarily because of luck. Luck is the most causally salient factor in her getting a true belief rather than a false one. Hence, according to the reply, Brenda doesn't perform an act of intellectual virtue after all. Had she performed a genuine act of intellectual virtue, luck would have been ruled out, and she would have gotten knowledge.[17]

This reply is promising, though it raises two further sets of questions. First, what does it mean for one causal factor to be more salient than another? Why is luck more salient than Brenda's intellectually virtuous actions and motivations? Why aren't her actions and motivations just as salient as luck, or more salient than luck? Second, does the reply beg the question against the Gettier problem? Does it merely stipulate that any act that is subject to the Gettier problem can't be a genuine act of intellectual virtue? Or, can we provide independent motivation for the fourth condition of an act of intellectual virtue?[18] Can we provide an analysis of causal saliency, or of an act of virtue, that doesn't beg the question against the Gettier problem? In answering these questions, we should explore independent analyses of causation, causal saliency, and acts of virtue – analyses that aren't motivated by solving the Gettier problem. We can look to metaphysics for independent analyses of causation, of which there are many. And we might look for independent analyses of acts of moral virtue in the literature on moral luck and virtue ethics. Ultimately, to determine whether this reply succeeds, we will need answers to the questions above.

But, in the meantime, there is good news. Suppose that examples like the one featuring Brenda do ultimately prevail – suppose that acts of intellectual virtue do prove to be *insufficient* for high-grade knowledge. What would this mean? It would merely mean that acts of intellectual virtue do not *always* result in high-grade knowledge. In the example above, Brenda performed an act of intellectual virtue, but lacked knowledge because luck still contributed to her getting a true belief. But, examples like these are bizarre and far-fetched – they are twisted. *Most* of the time, when we perform acts of intellectual virtue in the real world, we get true beliefs because of our intellectually virtuous actions and motives – luck has nothing to do with it. This means that *most* of the time, when we perform acts of intellectual virtue in the real world, we do get high-grade knowledge. To illustrate this point, let's transform the case above into something more realistic. Jane is a homicide detective, investigating the murder of an accountant. As before, there were no witnesses and there are two primary suspects: the CEO and the husband. This time, the CEO has recently been eviscerated in the local news for suspicious business transactions. Jane is aware of this, but she is also motivated to get the truth, to consider alternatives, and to carefully collect and evaluate evidence. Like the intellectually virtuous person, Jane collects the appropriate sort and amount of evidence, and thoroughly evaluates it. Despite the recent news, she does not jump to the conclusion that the CEO did it. Rather, she considers each suspect, in light of the evidence. This time, suppose that there is abundant and overwhelming evidence that points toward the husband. The evidence reveals (e.g.) that the husband despises his wife, that his prints are on the murder weapon, and that he told a friend that he wanted to arrange for his wife's demise. Accordingly, in evaluating the evidence, Jane comes to believe that the husband did it. Jane's belief is true. She also arrives at a true belief because of her intellectually virtuous actions and motives: if she hadn't done the same thing as a virtuous person – if she hadn't followed the evidence – then she wouldn't have gotten a true belief. There are no twists. Luck isn't a factor. In this case, Jane clearly performs an act an intellectual virtue. She shares the motives of the intellectually virtuous person, does what an intellectually virtuous person would do, and gets knowledge that the husband committed the murder as a result. The point is that in this case, and the many others like it (that arise in fields as diverse as medicine, economics, physics, and philosophy), performing an act of intellectual virtue does result in high-grade knowledge. Hence, even if acts of intellectual virtue are *not strictly sufficient* for high-grade knowledge, they still *usually* result in high-grade knowledge.

Are acts of intellectual virtue necessary for high-grade knowledge? Do we need to perform an act of intellectual virtue in order to get high-grade knowledge? Can you think of any cases where this is false – where we get high-grade knowledge without performing an act of intellectual virtue?

There are two good reasons to think that acts of intellectual virtue are not necessary for high-grade knowledge.

First, recall that acts of intellectual virtue require us to share the motivations of an intellectually virtuous person. These motivations are not innate. We must acquire them over time. And, they won't be easy to acquire. After all, an intellectually virtuous person hits the mean in her motivations. She consistently cares about truth appropriately, neither too little nor too much. Most of us care far too little about getting truth, and must work hard to care more. And, even when we succeed in caring more about truth on a single occasion, we often fail to do so consistently. So, most of us fall short of the motivations of an intellectually virtuous person. The problem is that if these motivations are required for high-grade knowledge, and most of us have not yet acquired them, then most of us won't have any high-grade knowledge. But, that seems wrong. Arguably, many of us (e.g., doctors, detectives, scientists, and students) have high-grade knowledge, even though we have not yet acquired the motivations of an intellectually virtuous person. To illustrate this point, suppose that a scientist is motivated by vanity, the desire to win the Nobel Prize, and "competitive opportunism" (Roberts and Wood 2007: 144). These motivations cause him to conduct a thorough investigation of a cutting-edge topic in his field, which, in turn, causes him to acquire true beliefs about that topic. The Opportunistic Scientist still does what an intellectually virtuous person would do – he thoroughly evaluates the evidence. But, his motivations fall short, and may even be vicious. He doesn't care about truth;[19] he cares about beating his competitors to publication, and about winning the Nobel Prize. And, yet, he still seems to acquire knowledge. Perhaps, this description fits James Watson and Francis Crick's discovery of the structure of DNA. Watson and Crick clearly acquired knowledge, even though their motivations fell short of the intellectually virtuous person's motivations.[20]

Second, recall that acts of intellectual virtue require us to do what an intellectually virtuous person would do. But is intellectually virtuous action required for high-grade knowledge? Don't we sometimes get high-grade knowledge without doing much of anything? Isn't high-grade knowledge the sort of thing that can be directly transferred from one person to another? Suppose that the Higgs-boson does indeed exist, and that scientists at the Large Hadron Collider (LHC) know this. They have high-grade knowledge that the Higgs-boson exists: their knowledge is the culmination of decades of active inquiry. You hear that the Higgs-boson exists while listening to the news. It seems that you now know that it exists, too. High-grade knowledge of its existence was transferred from the scientists at the LHC to millions of people around the world. But, *you* didn't conduct an active inquiry – somebody else did. Arguably, you did not have to do much of anything, let alone what a virtuous person would do. You just had the news on. Much of our knowledge comes from the testimony of others. Consider what we know about, for example, space, history, anthropology, disease, and the economy. Most of us are not actively engaged in exploring space, or in finding cures for diseases. And, yet we know a lot about discoveries in these fields. The epistemology of testimony is itself a burgeoning field. Some philosophers think that getting knowledge via testimony is an automatic and involuntary process, much like perception. Others think that getting knowledge via testimony requires active effort on our part – we need to evaluate who is, and is not, trustworthy. We won't attempt to decide this issue here.[21] But, if high-grade knowledge can be transmitted via testimony, and if getting high-grade knowledge via testimony is an involuntary process, then (arguably) an individual agent won't need to conduct an active inquiry herself – she won't need to *do* anything, let alone what an intellectually virtuous person would do – in order to get high-grade knowledge. She can get that knowledge from *someone else* who conducted an active inquiry.[22]

In sum, acts of intellectual virtue are *not strictly necessary* for high-grade knowledge. We don't *always* need to perform an act of intellectual virtue in order to get high-grade knowledge. But, in the real world, we still *sometimes* need to perform an act of intellectual virtue in order to get high-grade knowledge. At the boundaries of discovery, *somebody* needs to perform an active inquiry. When there are no witnesses to a murder, we can't get testimonial knowledge of the murderer's identity. Nor will we get such knowledge simply by opening our eyes at the crime scene. We have to conduct an investigation. In such situations, if we don't care about truth, and don't do what an intellectually virtuous person would do, then arguably we won't get knowledge (Battaly 2010b: 380–381). We can make the same point with different examples. For instance, knowing one's own sexual orientation sometimes requires the motivations and actions associated with the intellectual virtues of open-mindedness and care in gathering evidence. Contemporary society still pressures people to believe that they are heterosexual. This pressure can cause people who aren't heterosexual to ignore evidence, and jump to the conclusion that society favors. To combat this pressure, and avoid arriving at false beliefs about their own orientations, LGBT people may need to perform intellectually virtuous actions – for example, consider the possibility that they are not heterosexual, and weigh all of the evidence. Performing such actions will likely require a sufficiently strong motivation for truth. Without it, agents may succumb to the motive to believe whatever is easiest to believe. In short, this boundary of discovery sometimes requires the motivations and actions of an intellectually virtuous person (Battaly 2007). We can also borrow an example from Roberts and Wood. They argue that Jane Goodall could not have made her discoveries about chimps without intellectually virtuous motivations and actions. In their words, Goodall's love of animals motivated her to "spend vast amounts of time" with the chimps, which was "needed to garner the animals' trust, which in turn made it possible for her to observe things never before recorded by humans" (2007: 147).

So, why should we care about virtues? In the real world, doing what a virtuous person would do *often* results in right action and knowledge. It is also *often* needed to perform right acts and get knowledge. Since we presumably care about performing right acts, and getting knowledge, we should also care about doing what a virtuous person would do. In the next chapter, we consider whether virtues are necessary or sufficient for living well (flourishing).

6
Virtue and Living Well

Why should we care about virtues? So far, we have two reasons to care about the virtues that fall under our second key concept. First, if the views in Chapter 3 deliver on their promissory note, these virtues are valuable for their own sakes. Second, if Chapter 5 is correct, components of these virtues *often* result in right action and knowledge, and are *often* needed to perform right acts and get knowledge. Many philosophers think that there is a third important reason for caring about these virtues. They argue that these virtues are necessary or sufficient for *eudaimonia*. *Eudaimonia* is a concept that comes to us from Ancient Greek philosophy; it is sometimes translated as "happiness," at other times as "flourishing." Whatever the translation, philosophers agree that *eudaimonia* entails living and faring well. In other words, at minimum, *eudaimonia* involves living a life that benefits the person who leads it. The Stoics and, much more recently, Julia Annas have argued that the virtues are *sufficient* for *eudaimonia*.[1] They think that virtuous activity is enough for living and faring well – for leading a life that benefits the agent; nothing else is needed. In addition, the Stoics, Annas, and most philosophers who work on the virtues assume that the virtues are *necessary* for *eudaimonia*.[2] They think that a person cannot live well – she cannot lead a life that benefits her – without the virtues. If these claims are correct, then we have a third reason to care about the virtues: they are not just good for their own sakes and good for producing right action and knowledge; they are also good for the person who has them in a broader sense: they ensure that the person who has them leads a life that benefits her.

Are these claims correct? Are the virtues necessary or sufficient for living and faring well? This chapter suggests that they are neither. It argues that a person who possesses, and acts in accordance with, the virtues can still fail to lead a life that benefits her. To lead a life that benefits her, she must have some share of external goods, like freedom, health, and friendship. Consequently, virtue alone is *not sufficient* for living well. This chapter also suggests that a person can lead a life that benefits her without fully possessing the virtues. The virtues that fall under our second key concept are difficult to fully possess. We can fall short of these virtues without possessing vices; and can even fall short of them in fairly familiar ways. And yet, some of us who fall short of these virtues still fare well – we still lead lives that are good for us. Accordingly, virtue is *not necessary* for living well either.[3]

But, even if fully possessing the virtues isn't necessary for living well, those of us who live well are still likely to have some degree of virtue. This is because we aren't likely to have friends unless we have some degree of virtue; and, arguably, without friends, we won't live very well. So, we still have a third reason to care about, and try to develop, the virtues: without some degree of virtue, we aren't likely to live very well. Here, as in Chapter 5 above, degrees and components of virtue prove to be more germane than full virtue possession. Likewise, looser, probabilistic connections prove to be more important than necessary and sufficient ones.

6.1 Living Well: Some Parameters

The topic of living and faring well is complicated. Let's start by setting some parameters. First, to live well, a person must lead a life that is *good for* her. Though it may sound strange, there is a difference between claiming that the virtues are *good for* the people who have them, and claiming that the virtues are *good*. The virtues might be good, even though they aren't good for the people who have them. They might be good for some other reason – perhaps they are intrinsically good (see Chapter 3 above), or they are good for other people. To explicate: suppose we agree that virtues like benevolence, justice, and honesty are good. Few philosophers would dispute this claim; and all the major ethical theories endorse it (each for its own reasons). Despite this agreement, we can still legitimately disagree about whether these virtues are *good for* – whether they benefit – the people who have them. Some of us might think that these virtues are only *good for* – they only benefit – society; while others might think that these virtues benefit both society and the people who have them. The point is simply this: assuming that the virtues are good does not settle the issue of who or what they are good for. Unfortunately, the distinction between *good* and *good for* is obscured by Aristotle's use of "*eudaimonia*." Sometimes, Aristotle uses "*eudaimonia*" to mean a life that is *good for* the person who leads it. But, other times he uses it more broadly, to mean *the good life* – the life that is "lacking in nothing" and includes everything that is valuable (NE.1097b16). Here, we won't be disputing the claim that the virtues are *good*. Our working definition of virtue in Chapter 1 assumes that the virtues are good insofar as they are qualities that make us excellent people. Nor will we be disputing the claim that the virtues are part of the good life. If the views in Chapter 3 can deliver on their promissory note, then the virtues are intrinsically valuable, and thus part of the good life. But, we will dispute the claim that the virtues are necessary or sufficient for a life that is *good for* the person who leads it.[4] In simpler terms, we will dispute the claim that the virtues are necessary or sufficient for living well.

Second, whether a life is *good for* the person who leads it – whether one lives well – will be a matter of degree. The degree to which a person's life is good for her will lie somewhere along a broad continuum. For instance, a life may be very good for the person who leads it, just moderately good, or only slightly more good than bad. (Likewise, a life may be very bad, moderately bad, slightly more bad than good, and so on.) We won't try to specify exactly where any given life falls on this continuum. But, we will try to identify some lives that clearly fall in the good range (that clearly count as living well), and some lives that clearly fall in the bad range. In contrast, *the good life* does not admit of degrees. On Aristotle's view, the good life is "self-sufficient": it is the "most desirable of all things"; it "cannot become more desirable by the addition of anything to it" (NE.1097b15–17, 1172b31). Accordingly, it can't get any better than it already is; nor can it get worse.[5]

Aristotle ultimately argues that there is only one kind of life that counts as *the good life*: the life of contemplation (NE.X). Roughly, on his view, if you aren't a philosopher or mathematician, then you are disqualified from living the good life. But, this is clearly problematic; perhaps even more so when we move from the topic of *the good life* to our present topic: lives that are *good for* the people who lead them. Surely, a person need not be a philosopher or mathematician to live a life that is *good for* her. This would exclude all doctors, teachers, etc. from leading lives that benefit them; and is obviously too restrictive. Accordingly, third, we will assume that an agent need not be a philosopher to live well. Our theory should allow for more than one kind of life that is *good for* agents.[6]

6.2   Living Well: The Main Accounts

So, given these parameters, which lives are good for their agents? What does it take to live well? Our societies (especially in the United States) seem to value lives of pleasure and wealth above all else. But will lives of pleasure or wealth be enough?

Philosophers have focused on four main views about what it takes to live well. First, hedonists have argued that pleasure is indeed enough for living well. Roughly, if one experiences more pleasure than pain, and experiences high-quality pleasures (like intellectual pleasures), then one counts as living well. This would mean that living well is an experience – something entirely internal to us. But, is that correct? Robert Nozick has argued that it is not. In a famous thought-experiment, Nozick asks whether we would hook ourselves up to an experience machine. The machine would generate whatever experiences we wanted, even a "lifetime of bliss" (1977: 43). But we would be no more than bodies in tanks – imagine a happier version of *The Matrix* (Warner Bros., 1999). Would you hook yourself up to such a machine? Arguably, you wouldn't, or at least you shouldn't, since there is more to living well than what goes on inside our heads. Experiencing pleasure is not the only thing that matters. In addition to experiencing the love, comfort, and joy associated with friendships, we want to have real friendships, outside the machine. We want to act in ways that are, for example, kind and courageous, and we want to be kind and courageous. We won't accomplish any of these things if we are bodies are tanks.

Second, this has led some philosophers to argue that living well is a matter of satisfying our desires. Inside the experience machine, we have desires, but they don't actually get satisfied – for example, you don't graduate from college, even though you have the experience of graduating from college. According to desire-satisfaction views, a person leads a life that is good for her by actually getting what she wants; merely experiencing pleasure won't be enough. But, is getting what we want enough for living well? What if our desires are self-destructive? Consider the desires of drug addicts. Or, consider the desires of some of the girls whose stories are relayed in Kristof and WuDunn's *Half the Sky* (2009), which addresses sex trafficking in Southeast Asia. Kristof and WuDunn follow the lives of several girls who were sold to brothels in Cambodia. Some of those girls were able to escape the brothels to which they were sold; but of those who did escape, some wanted to return to the brothels – and succeeded in doing so.[7] On a much less serious note, I might want to quit my job, even though doing so would be very bad for me. In sum, an agent might want things that aren't good for her – we can be objectively wrong about what is good for us. Consequently, satisfying our desires won't be enough for living well either.

Third, some philosophers have argued for "objective-list" theories of living well. These views claim that living well is both subjective and objective. Accordingly, living well isn't just a matter of pleasure, or of desire-satisfaction. It also involves having some objective goods, like a sufficient degree of health, wealth, freedom, knowledge, friendship, family relationships, or perhaps other things, like a rewarding career. Objective-list theories typically claim that living well involves having some *combination* of these goods, along with pleasure and desire-satisfaction. So, they don't claim that, for example, wealth by itself is enough for living well. (Rich drug addicts who have ruined their health, careers, and relationships don't lead lives that benefit them.) But, this leads to a problem: it will be difficult to figure out which combination of goods goes on the list, and how much of those goods we need. Given our third parameter above, it will also be difficult to figure out how many acceptable lists there are. Interestingly, none of this makes objective-list theory false; it just makes it difficult to apply. (And, perhaps, it should be difficult to figure out which lives are good for us.) Objective-list theory also commits us to claiming that people can be wrong about what is good for them; and this may sound elitist. But, is it elitist to claim that people who are enslaved, or starving, or forced into prostitution, or addicted to meth are leading lives that are bad for them? Even if it is elitist, this doesn't mean that it is false. (Though, we should demonstrate humility in developing objective-list theories.)

Finally, some philosophers have argued that living well involves activity, specifically virtuous activity and virtue possession. These views argue that living well isn't a static state – it is not like earning a million dollars, or having 500 Facebook friends, or completing a triathlon. It is not the sort of thing that we can check off on a lifetime to-do list, and coast thereafter. Rather, living well consists in ongoing virtuous activity in our daily lives – continued open-mindedness, courage, and so on. If these views are correct, leading lives that good for us isn't a matter of amassing goods like wealth, health, and friendship. Instead, it is a matter of possessing virtues and acting in accordance with them, throughout our lifetimes. The remainder of this chapter addresses these views. It argues that possessing and acting in accordance with virtues is neither necessary nor sufficient for leading a life that is good for the agent. Still, we are likely to need some degree of virtue in order to live well, along with some share of goods like health, wealth, and friendship. In essence, this chapter suggests that we should combine objective-list theory with views that focus on virtue, while recognizing the limitations of necessary and sufficient conditions.

6.3 Is Virtue Sufficient for Living Well?

The Stoics argued that virtue is both necessary and sufficient for living well. In Cicero's words: "Wherefore as no wicked and foolish and idle man can have well-being, so the good and brave and wise man cannot be wretched" (1942: 19). In short, virtuous people cannot fail to lead lives that benefit them; whereas vicious people cannot possibly lead lives that benefit them. Is Cicero correct? Let's first explore whether virtue is *sufficient* for living well – whether virtuous people always lead lives that benefit them.

Epictetus – who was himself disabled, a slave, and later exiled – is one of the strongest proponents of the view that virtue is sufficient for living well. He argues that whether we live well depends on the way we *respond* to the circumstances we encounter. On his view, if we respond – if we act, feel, and think – in ways that are virtuous, then we are leading lives that benefit us. Nothing more is needed. In his forceful words: "What am I to be beheaded now . . .? Are you not willing to stretch out your neck, like Lanteranus at Rome, when Nero ordered him to be beheaded? For he stretched out his neck and took the blow, but when that blow was too weak, after shrinking back for a moment, he stretched out his neck again" (*Discourses* I.1.18–19) For Epictetus, botched beheadings do not detract from living well; nor does torture, imprisonment, illness, or the death of a child. Returning to his *Discourses*:

"Betray the secret."
I will not betray it; for this is in my own power.
"Then I will fetter you."
What are you saying, man? Fetter *me*? You will fetter my leg; but not even Zeus himself can get the better of my choice.
"I will cast you into prison."
My wretched body rather.
"I will behead you."

Did I ever tell you that I alone had a head that cannot be cut off?
(*Discourses* I.1.22–24)

On Epictetus's view, the only thing that detracts from living
well is the way we *respond* to the circumstances we find
ourselves in. The circumstances themselves do not detract
from (or add to) living well. So, if an agent responds badly
to, for example, being tortured – if he acts in ways that are
cowardly, or feels fear when he shouldn't – then he doesn't
lead a life that benefits him. But, if he responds virtuously to
being tortured, he does lead a life that benefits him, despite
the dire circumstances.

Epictetus holds this view because he thinks that human
beings are defined by our powers of reason – we are not our
bodies; rather, we are our faculties of choice. (Recall that in
fettering Epictetus's leg, one doesn't fetter Epictetus; in casting
his body into prison, one doesn't cast Epictetus into prison.)
Consequently, he thinks that we live and fare well as human
beings, when we choose and reason well; that is, when we
act, feel, and think virtuously. For Epictetus, whether we live
well or poorly is entirely internal to us. We can live well or
poorly, whatever our circumstances. Living well is also up to
us. We have control over whether our lives are good for us,
since we have control over the way we respond to our circumstances. The things we can't control – like illness, imprisonment, torture – are not part of living well; only the things
we can control – our actions and responses – are.

There are at least two appealing features of Epictetus's
view. First, it captures the idea that we can't control everything. We can control our actions and our reactions (to some
extent). But, we may not be able to control the circumstances
we are in. Our circumstances may be a result of luck. When
this happens, the Stoics have good advice: know what you
can and can't control, focus on what you can control, and
"let the rest go." In this vein, James Stockdale, a US Navy
pilot who was a prisoner of war in Vietnam, reports that
studying the Stoics helped him survive imprisonment and
torture. Second, relatedly, Epictetus's view captures the idea
that we can only do our best, given the circumstances we are
in. As Julia Annas explains the point: "living virtuously and
living happily are ways of . . . dealing with the materials I

have to hand, making the best of the life I have led up to now" (2011: 150). In short, it is not the circumstances that matter, but the way we cope with those circumstances. Epictetus's view is admirable. It may even be a correct view of what it takes to live in accordance with the virtues.[8] But, is it a correct view of living well? Arguably, it is not. One problem is that Epictetus, and the Stoics in general, overemphasize reason and choice. Granted, human beings are rational, and we should be partly identified with our powers of choice. But, we are also embodied. And, as a species, we are social. The Stoics overlook these features of our identities, which are vulnerable to bad luck and bad circumstances (Russell 2012). Second, according to Epictetus, our friends and families are not part of what make our lives good for us. In short, your best friend isn't part of what makes your life good for you; rather, what makes your life good for you is the way you respond to your best friend. But this seems egotistical and counterintuitive.

Third, there is a difference between making the best of a life, and leading a life that is good for the agent. Consider some further examples from *Half the Sky*. Kristof and WuDunn report that women and girls in Kasturba Nagar, India and in rural Ethiopia are routinely subjected to kidnapping and rape. Some are publicly gang-raped; others are repeatedly kidnapped and raped. Some of these women and girls respond with courage – they report the rapes to police, despite the fact that rape is stigmatizing (in identifying themselves as victims of rape, they risk expulsion from their communities). But, some of those same courageous women have been subsequently gang-raped by the very police officers to whom they report the crimes. I submit that though they are virtuous, and though they are making the best of their circumstances, these women are clearly leading lives that are bad for them. Perhaps, had they not been virtuous, they would be leading lives that were even worse for them. That is a separate point (addressed in the next section). Here, the point is that being virtuous, by itself, isn't enough to make their lives good for them – it isn't enough to make their lives fall in "the good range." So, Epictetus's view is wrong. Virtue isn't sufficient for living well; living well requires at least some good circumstances.

It is important to note that the women and girls above cannot be blamed for leading lives that are bad for them. They cannot, by themselves, control their circumstances. Epictetus is right about that. Nevertheless, those circumstances – here, especially, lack of freedom – do make their lives bad for them. Epictetus got this point wrong. It is not entirely up to us whether we live well; luck makes a contribution. Arguably, any of us could have been born into the circumstances described above. We are lucky that we weren't; and the women above are unlucky that they were.

Lack of freedom isn't the only circumstance that has the potential to make a life bad for the person who lives it. Severe poverty, resulting in a lack of consistent access to food, water, and medicine, can make a life bad; as can severe illness and pain. Arguably, even a lack of close personal relationships has the potential to make a life bad. (This explains why solitary confinement is a punishment.) Epictetus recognizes that specific individuals may not be able to control their circumstances – their lack of freedom, or lack of access to food and medicine. But, he overlooks the power that communities have over circumstances. Once we, as a community, recognize that severe poverty, illness, and oppression contribute to living poorly, we can help change those circumstances, and help make people's lives better for them.

Aristotle has similar reasons for thinking that virtue is insufficient for living well. In his words: "Those who say that the victim on the rack or the man who falls into great misfortunes is [living well] if he is [virtuous], are . . . talking nonsense" (NE.1153b19–20). On Aristotle's view, human beings are rational; but we are also embodied, and our bodies "must be healthy and must have food and other attention" (NE.1178b34). To lead lives that are good for us as humans, we must have a share of "external goods" (NE.1099a32). Which external goods? And how much of them do we need? In addition to health, Aristotle thinks we need things like: friends, wealth, political power, leisure time, and "good birth, satisfactory children, [and] beauty" (NE.1099b2). How much of these things do we need to live well? Do we need to be uber-rich and drop-dead gorgeous? Aristotle argues that living well requires a moderate share of external goods. In his words: "we must not think the man who is to be happy

will need many things or great things . . . for self-sufficiency
and action do not depend on excess, and we can do noble
acts without ruling earth and sea; for even with moderate
advantages one can act excellently" (NE.1178b34–1179a5).
In other words, we don't need to have maximal shares of
these things in order to live well; we just need to have enough
of them. We don't need to be uber-wealthy; we just need to
be wealthy enough. How much wealth is enough? Aristotle
doesn't specify; and, given our second parameter above,
neither will we. It is difficult to evaluate lives in the middle
of the continuum – it is difficult to say exactly which lives
are slightly more good than bad, and which are slightly more
bad than good. But, we can at least say the following: lives
that are clearly in the good range involve having enough
wealth to access food, water, and medicine. To the extent that
poverty prevents a person from consistently accessing these
goods, it makes her life bad for her.

Do we need a share of each of the above things in order
to live well? Or will a share of some, but not all, of them be
enough? Aristotle seems to think that we need a share of each
of the above things. There are two reasons to be wary of this.
First, even if we agree that we need a share of wealth, we
might object to some of the other things on Aristotle's list.
Granted, beautiful people seem to have easier lives than the
rest of us, but do we really need a share of beauty to live
well? Do we need to have children? Can't childless people
lead lives that are good for them? This raises a broader issue:
it is difficult to determine which things belong on the list, and
why. Do political power, education, and a rewarding career
belong on the list? Do things belong on the list because of
who we are as human beings? If so, we will need to develop
an account of the features that we share as human beings. As
we said in section 6.2, these issues make objective-list theory
complicated, but they don't necessarily make it false. Figuring
out which lives are good for us should be complicated.

Second, we will also need to consider how many different
lists there are. There are some features of humanity that we
all share. Hence, we can expect there to be some things that
we all need to live well – some things that will appear on all
of our lists – for example, enough health, wealth, freedom,
and social interaction. (We'll need social interaction provided

that human beings are social.) But, we are also individuals with different desires, goals, likes, and dislikes. So, we can expect our lists to diverge somewhat. For instance, in addition to needing enough health, wealth, etc., some people may also need children in order to lead lives that are good for them. (They may emphatically want children, may be miserable without them, etc.) But, other people may not. The point is that our version of objective-list theory allows for the possibility that different individuals may need different combinations of things to live well. Following our third parameter, it allows for more than one kind of life that is good for agents.

If this version of objective-list theory is correct, then living well is not entirely up to us. Having enough health, wealth, and freedom are factors over which we have little control. Had I been born 100 years earlier in the United States, I would not have had the right to vote (US women did not acquire that right until 1919). Had any of us been born as women in rural Ethiopia today, we would be subject to kidnapping and rape. When and where one is born, the family into which one is born, and the resources of that family are all matters of luck. The proposed view recognizes this. If it is correct, it gives us a reason to help improve living conditions around the world, so that more people can reach the thresholds of health, wealth, and freedom that are needed for living well.

6.4   Is Virtue Necessary for Living Well?

Even though Aristotle thinks that we need external goods in order to live well, he does not think that having external goods will be enough for living well. On his view, living well also requires that we possess and act in accordance with the virtues. Most philosophers who work on the virtues agree with this point – they think that the virtues are necessary for living well.[9] In short, they think that having stuff (like wealth, health, etc.) isn't enough. Living well also depends on what we *do* with the stuff that we have. To explicate: suppose the argument above is correct, and we each need a share of wealth, health, freedom, and social interaction in order to live well. That is, we each need enough of these goods to put us over the threshold – to put our lives into the good range on the continuum. But many of us, whose lives have far-and-away cleared that threshold, continue to amass stuff. Just consider how many cell phones, or gourmet meals, you have purchased in the last five years. The argument is that we can use this extra stuff well or badly. Using it badly produces lives that are not good for their agents, and using it well requires the virtues.[10] To illustrate: if we aren't temperate, we will use food, drink, and sex badly – we will overindulge, and thus erode our health. If we aren't benevolent, we will treat our friends and family badly, and thus erode our relationships. If we aren't generous and just, we won't donate enough money or time to legitimate causes, and will lead lives akin to that of Ebenezer Scrooge. Daniel Russell even argues that we can use love badly, by becoming obsessed with the beloved person and ignoring all our other relationships (2012: 69). To sum up this line of thought, in the words of Julia Annas: "a big house, a car, money, holidays don't make us happy if we cannot make the right use of them in our lives . . . our happiness comes at least in part from the way we . . . actively live our lives" (2011: 151–152). It comes, at least in part, from virtuous activity.

Is this correct? Is virtue required for leading lives that are good for us? Let's consider two different questions. First, can vicious people lead lives that are good for them? And, second, can people who fall short of fully possessing the virtues lead lives that are good for them? (Recall, from Chapter 4, that one can fall short of fully possessing virtues, while also failing to fully possess vices.) If we answer either question in the affirmative, then virtue is not necessary for living well.

Stephen Cahn's "The Happy Immoralist" argues that vicious people can lead lives that benefit them. Cahn asks us to consider Fred, who is "treacherous and thoroughly dishonest," and who has devoted his life solely to acquiring fame, money, and reputation (2004: 1). Fred is not interested in friends or truth, but he has attained his goals. He is a "rich celebrity renowned for his supposed integrity," who experiences "great pleasure" (2004: 1). Cahn argues that Fred is leading a life that is good for him. Is Cahn correct? There are at least two problems with the way Cahn has described Fred. First, Fred doesn't have friends. But, if human beings are social, then we will all need some friends, or other close personal relationships, in order to lead lives that are good for us. In other words, we need some personal relationships in order to put us over the threshold. A similar problem arises for Patrick Bateman, the protagonist of Bret Easton Ellis's 1991 novel *American Psycho*. Bateman is clearly vicious, but doesn't live well in part because he lacks friends. Second, Cahn seems to think that experiencing pleasure and satisfying one's desires is enough for living well. But, section 6.2 above argues against this: we wouldn't hook ourselves up to Nozick's experience machine, and we might desire things that are bad for us. This too applies to Bateman.

Daniel Haybron (2008: 159–160) offers a slightly better example: Genghis Khan. Khan is known for founding the Mongolian Empire, and directing the ruthless slaughter of millions in the process. Khan was clearly vicious. Khan also clearly had power and wealth, and is reported to have had some friends, and some interest in learning from philosophy and religion. Still, we might question whether Khan's life was good for him. Though born into nobility, Khan grew up in relative poverty. His wife was kidnapped. He was betrayed by a close friend (whom he later had killed) and, on a separate occasion, by one of his own sons (whom he is reputed to have had poisoned). Another of his sons died in battle, and Khan himself was reported to have been wounded in battle. So, arguably, Khan's life wasn't very good for him.

Perhaps, we will have more success generating our own examples of vicious people who lead lives that are good for them. Consider, for instance, Roger Sterling, who is a partner in the advertising firm Sterling Cooper on the television series *Mad Men* (AMC, 2007–15). As was argued in Chapter 4, Sterling has the vice of self-indulgence – he consumes alcohol and sex excessively. He is also frequently dishonest and unjust. And, yet, he seems to lead a life that is good for him. He clearly has enough wealth, freedom, and power. He is also healthy, despite his excesses, and even has a friend who shares the same excesses, Don Draper. Alternatively, consider the characters in the 2001 film, *Ocean's Eleven* (Warner Bros.).

The characters, including Danny Ocean and Rusty Ryan, are crooks and con-men. They make a living by conducting multi-million dollar heists. They are arguably dishonest and unjust. And, yet, they lead lives that are reasonably good for them – they are wealthy, healthy, and only spend limited time behind bars. Perhaps, most importantly, they are clearly friends with one another.

What should we say of cases like these, in which vicious people seem to have friends who are also vicious? There are three worries about these cases. First, one might worry that Sterling and Draper aren't really friends. They are just co-workers and drinking buddies. They don't really trust each other, or confide in each other. One might even argue that Sterling has no genuine relationships at all. Consequently, one might conclude that Sterling's life really isn't good for him – his wealth, heath, and power aren't enough to put his life over the threshold. To lead a life that is good for him, he needs at least one genuine relationship. Second, one might worry that Ocean and Ryan aren't fully vicious. They are dishonest in many contexts, but not in all contexts – they don't lie to, or betray, each other. They are, as it were, "gentleman thieves." So, even though their lives are good for them, they aren't completely vicious. Notice that these responses suggest an inverse correlation between possessing vice and having friends. The more vicious a person is (Sterling), the less likely he is to have friends. And, the closer a person's relationships are (Ocean), the less likely he is to be fully vicious. Finally, one might object that these examples are only fictional. In real life, it is difficult to find examples of people who are fully vicious, and yet have the friends they need in order to lead lives that are good for them.

Suppose, for the moment, that these examples fail – we haven't successfully identified a vicious person who lives well. Would it then follow that we need the virtues in order to live well? Not necessarily. After all, as was pointed out in Chapter 4, we could fall short of fully possessing the virtues, while also failing to fully possess the vices. So, to show that the virtues are not necessary for living well, we could instead look for examples in which people fall short of the virtues, but still live well. As we will see, these cases are easier to generate, and are more familiar.

Recall that to fully possess the virtue of benevolence, one must consistently perform a particular kind of action – one must consistently help others when it is appropriate to do so – and one must consistently care about the well-being of others. To fully possess the virtue of justice, one must consistently treat others with respect, and one must consistently care about the autonomy of others. We fall short of fully possessing these virtues when we only help and respect people who are like us, or who are in our own group. In Nancy Snow's insightful words, we fall short when our "virtues do not extend beyond . . . members of [our] . . . group" (2008: 238). Those of us who only help and respect people we know are neither fully benevolent nor fully just.

Consider, for instance, the *Homophobic Parent*. Imagine an older, healthy, affluent, American banker, who enjoys his work, adores his children, values education, and makes charitable donations. He pays for his children to attend college, and regularly donates money to animal shelters in his community. As a banker, he also issues loans to independent businesses in his community. He still has close personal relationships with several of his friends from college, he enjoys spending time with his co-workers, and he loves his wife, children, and pets. He consistently cares about, helps, and respects his friends and family, and the people in his own community. He has a degree of the virtues of benevolence and justice – he isn't fully vicious. But, he does not care about, help, or respect homosexuals, whom he views as degenerate outsiders. He doesn't go out of his way to persecute gays and lesbians; but he fails to help and respect them when such opportunities arise (for example, he rejects loans for projects that he thinks support "a gay agenda"). His friends, wife, and community are similarly homophobic. I submit that the Homophobic Parent falls short of fully possessing the virtues of benevolence and justice. Those virtues require consistently helping and respecting others, even (and perhaps especially) others who are different from oneself. And, yet, the Homophobic Parent arguably leads a life that is good for him, perhaps even very good for him. Within his isolated community, he has wealth, health, power, some degree of virtue, close personal relationships, and a job he enjoys and finds meaningful. (Analogously, we can generate a Racist Parent who lives well.)

Relatedly, consider an example generated by Marilyn Friedman (and cited by Snow), the *Sexist Patriarch*. Friedman imagines a family man who believes that men are superior to women. The Sexist Patriarch does not view women as equals. But nor is he hostile toward women. He "may sincerely love them in the same way that any adult might love a young child who is dependent on his . . . protection and guidance" (Friedman 2009: 36). Situate the Sexist Patriarch in the United States in the 1950s; and imagine that he is wealthy, healthy, powerful, educated (as it were), and enjoys a meaningful career. He also cares about, helps, and respects the men in his life, all of whom are wealthy, healthy, powerful, and share his views about the inferiority of women. He has close friendships with several of these men. But, he does not respect the women in his life, nor does he consistently help them. Though he protects and guides the women in his life, he does not care about them as individuals or support their projects when they differ from his. I submit that the Sexist Patriarch clearly falls short of possessing the virtues of benevolence and justice, but still leads a life that is good for him, perhaps very good for him.

More generally, many of us probably fall short of full virtue possession. There will be some groups of people that we do not care about or respect as much as we should. For instance, as college students and professors, we may not have enough respect for the people who work for us – who do the gardening at our universities, who serve us lunch in the cafeteria, who clean our classrooms, offices, and dormitories. And, yet, as college students and professors, we may care about and respect a great many people. We may be closer to full virtue possession than either the Homophobic Parent or the Sexist Patriarch, though we still fall short. And, we may simultaneously lead lives that are good for us. Many of us are healthy, and wealthy enough to afford an education. We enjoy intellectual pleasures, and have close friendships.

It is easier to fall short of virtue than it is to fully possess vice. We may recognize the three characters above in some of the people in our own lives, or in ourselves. Notice that each of them has a degree of virtue. Each is benevolent and just, when it comes to the people in his or her own group. The Homophobic Parent is benevolent and just with respect to heterosexuals; the Sexist Patriarch with respect to men; and college students and professors with respect to many people, but not working-class people on our own campuses. As Nancy Snow puts the point, each has virtues that are "limited in scope" (2008: 235). This may make it easier to believe that each has friends – friends whose virtues are likewise limited in scope. As we saw above, it may be harder to believe that fully vicious people have friends. After all, the person who fully possesses the vice of self-indulgence (Roger Sterling) will be a selfish pleasure-seeker across the board; and the person who fully possesses the vice of cruelty (Genghis Khan) will be cruel across the board. Granted, *we* would not be friends with Roger Sterling or Genghis Khan – we would correctly judge them to be treating us badly, and would not tolerate such treatment. But, we are not fully vicious. It is difficult to say whether fully vicious people could have friends who are themselves fully vicious.

Either way, we have shown that full virtue possession is not necessary for living well. If vicious people like Sterling really can have friends, then not even a degree of virtue will be necessary for living well. And, if vicious people like Sterling really can't have friends, then the Homophobic Parent, the Sexist Patriarch, and the college students and professors described above still can. They all live well, while falling short of full virtue possession.

In sum, what can we conclude about the connections between virtue and living well? First, full virtue possession is not sufficient for living well. Second, full virtue possession is not necessary for living well. But, interestingly, the discussion above also suggests a third conclusion. Even though full virtue possession is not strictly necessary for living well, there seems to be a looser connection between having friends and having some degree of virtue. In short, we aren't *likely* to have friends unless we have some degree of virtue. Granted, it may be *possible* for fully vicious people to have fully vicious friends. But, even if this is possible, it is not the standard case. In the real world, most of us do not fully possess the vices. We fall somewhere in between fully possessing the vices and fully possessing the virtues. Accordingly, the less benevolent, just, and honest we are, the less likely we are to have friends and close relationships. Perhaps, we will eventually be able to empirically test this hypothesis. If philosophers and psychologists work together to design measures for the virtues, and measures for friendship, then we will be able to test it. For now, we have a third reason to care about, and try to develop, the virtues: without some degree of virtue, we aren't likely to have friends or close relationships, and without friends or close relationships, we won't live well. All told, we have three reasons to care about the virtues that fall under our second key concept. If the views in Chapter 3 deliver on their promissory note, these virtues are intrinsically valuable. If Chapter 5 is correct, components of these virtues *often* result in right action and knowledge, and are *often* needed to perform right acts and get knowledge. And, if this chapter is correct, without some degree of these virtues, we aren't likely to live well.

7
How Can We Acquire the Virtues?

According to the second key concept, virtues are acquired character traits. Previous chapters have given us several incentives to develop such virtues. They have claimed that the virtues are intrinsically valuable, that they often produce right action and knowledge, and that we aren't likely to live very well without (some degree of) them. But, we have also seen that such virtues are difficult to acquire. They involve consistent patterns of action, and stable motivations, both of which we must learn over time. So, now that we have sufficient incentive to acquire these virtues, how do we go about doing so? How can we acquire the virtues?

This chapter suggests that we acquire the virtues via habituation. In other words, we develop the patterns of action and motivation, which are necessary for the virtues, via practice and imitation. We imitate the actions and motives of people who have, or are closer to having, the virtues than we are. This suggestion is hardly new. There is a long tradition of arguing that the moral virtues are acquired via habituation, dating back to the ancients. What is new is the application of this idea to the acquisition of intellectual virtues in university classrooms.[1] This chapter suggests several activities that we can use in university classrooms to help our students (and ourselves) get closer to acquiring intellectual virtues.

7.1 Habituation

In Plato's early dialogues, Socrates argues that acquiring moral virtues is relatively easy – we need only acquire knowledge of which acts a virtuous person would perform. In *Protagoras*, Socrates claims that "knowledge is a fine thing quite capable of ruling a man . . . if he can distinguish good from evil, nothing will force him to act otherwise than as knowledge dictates" (352c). In other words, once you know which acts are virtuous, you will (barring external impediments) perform those virtuous acts. For Socrates, motivations and desires can conflict with our knowledge of which acts we should perform. But, those motivations and desires are incapable of overpowering our knowledge. Acquiring knowledge is sufficient for acquiring moral virtue (see Battaly 2014b).

Plato's later dialogues, like *Republic*, and Aristotle's *Nicomachean Ethics* tell a different story. Both Plato and Aristotle argue for a tripartite soul, in which it is possible for motivations and desires to not only conflict with knowledge, but overpower it. This means that knowledge of which acts are virtuous isn't enough to get us to do them. Competing emotions and motivations can prevent us from performing virtuous acts. Recall, from Chapter 4, the *akratic* person, who suffers from weakness of will. In Aristotle's words, the *akratic* person does know what he should do, but he fails to use this knowledge, and instead performs bad acts "as a result of passion" (NE.1145b12). The *akratic* knows what he should do, and is even motivated to do it, but his competing motivations are too strong and prevent him from doing it. For Plato and Aristotle, we won't acquire dispositions to perform virtuous actions, and thus won't acquire the virtues, unless we train our motivations and desires so that they are consistent with our knowledge.

How do we do that? Plato and Aristotle both argue that our motivations and desires must be habituated from childhood. In Aristotle's words, "it is on account of . . . pleasure that we do bad things, and on account of . . . pain that we abstain from noble ones. Hence we ought to have been brought up in a particular way from our very youth, as Plato says, so as both to delight in and to be pained by the things that we ought" (NE.1104b10–13). In short, both think that, as children and throughout our lives, we ought to imitate and practice the actions and motivations of virtuous people. Accordingly, in *Republic*, Plato argues that the future guardians should only be encouraged to imitate exemplars of virtue, never of vice, since "imitations practiced from youth become part of nature and settle into habits of gesture, voice, and thought" (395d). This is why only virtuous music, poetry, and stories are allowed into Plato's *polis*. Relatedly, Aristotle argues that to acquire the virtues, we must practice the actions of virtuous people: just as "men become builders by building and lyre-players by playing the lyre; so too we become just by doing just acts, temperate by doing temperate acts, brave by doing brave acts" (NE.1103a33–34). He thinks that children, and even adults, can imitate virtuous acts – they can do the same thing that a virtuous person would do – long before they have fully acquired the virtues. To illustrate: a child may initially do what is just – for example, share toys with her brother – because her parents have promised her an independent reward, not because she respects her brother and values fairness. Aristotle seems to think that dispositions of virtuous action and virtuous motivation develop in tandem. Roughly, by repeatedly practicing just acts, and earning independent rewards for doing so, a person will come to associate pleasure with those acts and will want to do them. Gradually, she will develop the intrinsic motivation to respect others for their own sake.

In contemporary virtue ethics, the leading analysis of habituation is Nancy Sherman's. In *The Fabric of Character* (1989), Sherman argues that we acquire moral virtues by practicing the actions, emotions, and perceptions of exemplars; and by listening to their explanations. She thinks that by repeatedly trying on virtuous actions, emotions, and perceptions, we develop a taste for them; roughly, by practicing virtuous actions, we cement our motivations to perform them. For Sherman, habituation is not a matter of mindless repetition – we don't repeat the very same behavior over and over again. Rather, we try to get increasingly closer to the actions, emotions, and perceptions of our exemplars by noting the degree to which each of our own attempts succeeds or fails to reach that ideal. On Sherman's view, exemplars also do more than simply serve as models to be imitated. Exemplars direct us to perform specific actions (e.g., to help this person, rather than ignore her), to size up situations in specific ways (e.g., to see this as an opportunity for benevolence, rather than gloating), and to have specific emotions and motivations (e.g., to feel compassion and care for the person). In an effort to eventually make us self-sufficient, they also provide explanations of their actions, which we can use to improve our own efforts. In sum, according to Sherman, habituation involves practice and imitation on our part, and explanation and guidance on the part of exemplars (see Battaly 2006: 205).

Zagzebski applies these insights to contemporary virtue epistemology, arguing that intellectual virtues are also acquired via habituation. On her view, both the moral virtues and the intellectual virtues develop in stages. Those stages: "begin with the imitation of virtuous persons, require practice which develops certain habits of feeling and acting, and usually include an in-between stage of intellectual self-control (overcoming intellectual *akrasia*)" (1996: 150). To illustrate: for Zagzebski, the first stage of acquiring the virtue of open-mindedness seems to consist in practicing the acts and motivations of an open-minded person. So, the agent would practice considering alternative ideas; initially because she wanted to please her mentor or get an external reward, and eventually because she desired the truth for its own sake. The second stage seems to be marked by intellectual *akrasia*, whereby the agent knows that she should consider alternative ideas and is motivated to do so, but fails to do so because of competing motivations (e.g., the motivation to believe what she already believes). In the third stage, she is *enkratic* (see Chapter 4 above). She still has competing motivations, but they are weaker, and outweighed by her motivation to care about the truth for its own sake. Accordingly, she succeeds in consistently considering alternative ideas. Finally, the agent acquires the virtue of open-mindedness when her motivation for truth has become strong enough to eliminate competing motivations – when she no longer has to struggle to consider alternative ideas (see Battaly 2006: 204).

According to all these analyses of habituation, we acquire virtues via repetition, guided practice, and the imitation of exemplars (who explain their actions and motivations). The idea of acquiring consistent patterns of *action* through practice and imitation will be familiar enough. After all, this is precisely how we acquire a wide range of skills – everything from driving a car to hitting cross-court forehands. But, the idea of acquiring intrinsic *motivations* via practice and imitation will be less familiar, and a bit mysterious. The final section suggests some extracurricular activities (for example, participating in Philosophy Clubs) that might help students acquire intrinsic motivations, like the motivation to pursue the truth for its own sake. But this is clearly an area that warrants further exploration, both by philosophers and educational psychologists.

7.2   Objections

There are several worries about habituation as a method of acquiring the virtues. First, one might worry that habituation is little more than indoctrination – that it is no better than the brainwashing of a cult. There is a ready reply to this objection. For starters, the virtues themselves are mindful habits, not mindless ones. To illustrate, the open-minded person doesn't respond to every situation with the same action. If she did, open-mindedness would be much easier to acquire than it is. Instead, she learns to stand-at-the-ready in a particular way – to be alert for opportunities to consider alternative ideas, and once she has perceived those opportunities, to judge whether and to what degree she should consider them. Unlike an automaton with canned responses, the open-minded person recognizes that each situation must be judged on its own merits – that it is neither always right to consider alternatives, nor always wrong to ignore them. The goal of habituation is to enable us to make these judgments, and choose the appropriate actions, on our own. So, in practicing virtuous actions, we don't mindlessly repeat the same behavior, as we do when learning to brush our teeth. Instead, we size up situations, judge which actions to perform, and evaluate whether our attempts at virtuous action matched those of our exemplars. Likewise, in providing guidance and explanation for their actions and motivations, our exemplars are not trying to brainwash us; they are trying to help us make critical evaluations on our own.

Second, according to the descriptions of habituation above, developing extrinsic motivations for external rewards can help us develop the intrinsic motivations that are required for the virtues. As the story above goes, we may initially learn to perform virtuous acts because we are promised external rewards, not because we value others, or the truth, for their own sakes. According to the above, these external rewards will give us pleasure, which we will associate with the virtuous acts we perform, thus motivating us to do them. Gradually, this process is supposed to help us develop intrinsic motivations: we are supposed to eventually come to care about others, or the truth, for their own sakes. The *problem* is that stories like this have been contested in the recent psychological literature on intrinsic motivation and external reward in education.[2] There is mounting evidence that extrinsic motivation for tangible rewards (e.g., money, awards) does not facilitate, and even undermines, intrinsic motivation. According to Edward Deci, Richard Koestner, and Richard Ryan, a host of psychological studies have shown that offering students tangible rewards for tasks like reading and writing actually *decreases* their intrinsic motivation to perform such tasks.[3] Deci et al. found these effects to be particularly pronounced for schoolchildren, and still clearly significant (though less pronounced) for college students. Deci et al. also briefly address the effects of external reward on tasks which students had no prior intrinsic motivation to perform (and thus none to decrease). They found that offering students tangible rewards got them to perform these tasks, but did not help them develop any intrinsic motivation to do so. What does appear to facilitate intrinsic motivation, at least for college students, is positive verbal feedback. There is no easy reply to this objection. If Deci et al. are correct, then the account of habituation above is (at best) incomplete.[4] It should be updated to include the latest psychological research on the facilitators of intrinsic motivation.

Third, as described above, habituation involves the imitation of exemplars – of people who possess the virtues. But, what if the virtues are so difficult to acquire that very few, or none, of us possess them? What if none of us are exemplars? Recall the situationist objection from Chapter 3. Situationists have argued that virtues, as described by our second key concept, are so hard to get that few, or none, of us have them – that there just aren't exemplars around for us to imitate. Are situationists correct?[5] As we saw in Chapter 3, John Doris and Gilbert Harman use studies in social psychology to argue for two claims. First, they argue for (what I will call) "weak situationism": the view that trivial changes in one's situation can influence whether one performs virtuous actions. Second, they argue that whether we perform virtuous actions – whether we do what the virtuous person would do – depends on what type of situation we are in; for example, if we are running late, we won't help the people we should; but if we are early, we will. In short, they contend that our actions vary in accordance with changes in our situations. If so, we won't perform virtuous actions across a wide range of different situations, as is required by global virtues. Accordingly, Doris and Harman endorse a second conclusion, (what I will call) "strong situationism": the view that most, or even all, people lack global virtues. Few, perhaps none, of us are exemplars.

   In reply, the studies cited by Doris and Harman arguably don't support strong situationism, but do support weak situationism. In other words, the studies succeed in showing that situations can independently influence our actions. This is revelatory. It means that we don't have as much control over our actions as we might have thought. It also means that our actions are not always the products of character traits; sometimes they are the products of situations. But, the studies do not show that strong situationism is true. For starters, they don't show that our actions are always the products of situations. They don't show that situations are the sole determinants of action. If they were, then the subjects in each study should have all behaved the same way, since they were all in the same situation. But they didn't all behave the same way – recall that approximately 35 percent of Milgram's subjects balked. Nor do the studies directly support the claim that most people lack global virtues. They provide some indirect evidence for that claim, but direct evidence would involve longitudinal studies, which follow the same subject across different situations. Importantly, most of the studies Doris and Harman cite are *not* longitudinal – they don't track subjects from one situation to the next (Doris 2002: 38, 121). In short, situationists are partly correct. They are right about weak situationism, but wrong about strong situationism. What does this mean? What are the implications for virtues, their acquisition, and exemplars? Are exemplars as scarce as situationists think? Arguably, this means that both character traits *and* situations can cause our actions. Character traits and situations often work together to cause our actions, but can sometimes cause our actions independently. Roughly, the idea is that weak situationism does not preclude us from acquiring *nearly* global virtues. To possess *nearly* global virtues, we must perform virtuous actions in a wide range of situations. And to do that, we must learn to overcome a wide range of situational impediments. Accordingly, virtues won't be local in the way that Doris suggests – they will be broader than Doris's local virtue of "being-early-benevolence." But, importantly, they won't be maximally global in the way that the second key concept suggests either. Instead, virtues will issue appropriate actions in a wide variety of situations, but not in every situation. To illustrate, a person who fails to help others in distress because she is in a hurry, or in a neutral mood, or in a group will not have the virtue of benevolence. To have that virtue, she must produce virtuous actions in a wide range of situations – helping others only when she is early isn't enough. But she need not produce virtuous actions in *every* situation. This is where contemporary virtue theory should pay attention. Claiming that virtues must issue virtuous actions in *every* situation is tantamount to denying that situations can independently influence our actions. But, it is naive to think that character-building could enable us to overcome *every* situational influence. If weak situationism is true, it can't: our actions are not always the products of character traits. Of course, the trick is figuring out *which* situational influences we need to overcome in order to have nearly global virtues; and which situational influences we can't overcome. On this point, we can learn from Sosa and Driver, both of whom index the virtues to conditions.[6] Recall, from Chapter 2, that Sosa indexes the virtue of vision to conditions in which we see nearby objects, in good

for helping students develop intellectual virtues in university classrooms. According to the second key concept, those virtues involve dispositions of action and motivation. Hence, the strategies below provide students with opportunities to practice: (1) *identifying* intellectually virtuous actions and motivations; and (2) *performing* intellectually virtuous actions, and *having* intellectually virtuous motivations. Admittedly, the suggestions below are incomplete – for instance, they do not solve the problem of how to acquire intrinsic motivations. Nor are they guaranteed to succeed. But they do get us started. As faculty, we can expect the activities and assignments below to help our students make progress in acquiring intellectual virtues.

Habituation, as we saw above, is not mindless. To acquire intellectual virtues, students must learn to (1) identify, and evaluate, intellectual actions and motivations (so as to eventually make such judgments on their own). They must learn to discern which intellectual actions and motivations are virtuous, which are not, and why. As faculty, we can help students do this. For starters, we can introduce them to a wide range of intellectual actions and motivations, explaining which are intellectually virtuous, which aren't, and why. As we saw in Chapter 3, intellectual actions are, roughly, the actions an agent performs in acquiring beliefs or conducting inquiries. They include: generating hypotheses, weighing evidence, ignoring evidence, searching for evidence, jumping to conclusions, following through on leads, considering alternative ideas, ignoring alternative ideas, entertaining objections, ignoring objections, defending one's view against objections, and conceding that another's view is correct. Depending on the context, some of these actions will be virtuous, others won't. Intellectual motivations are, roughly, the agent's motivations for performing these actions. They include: the motivation for truth, the motivation to believe whatever makes one feel good, the motivation to believe whatever is easiest, the motivation to believe whatever will win one an award, and the motivation to believe whatever will get one a promotion or a good grade. According to Chapter 3, the motivation for truth, or more broadly "cognitive contact with reality" (Zagzebski 1996: 167), is intellectually virtuous; the other motivations are not.

As faculty, we can also acquaint students with the actions and motivations that are characteristic of the individual intellectual virtues. The virtues of open-mindedness and intellectual courage readily lend themselves to this purpose. As we saw in Chapter 3, the open-minded person characteristically considers alternative ideas; while the intellectually courageous person characteristically stands up for her beliefs. Both are motivated to get the truth for its own sake.

The examples of intellectual action and motivation that we introduce to students need not come from our own lives. They can be the actions and motivations of others, fictional or real. In this vein, it will be useful to expose students to exemplars, or near exemplars, of intellectual virtue (see the example from *House M.D.* below). But, it will also be useful to expose them to a range of intellectual actions and motivations, some of which are virtuous, and others of which are not. Doing so will help students learn to identify which actions a virtuous person would, and would not, perform. The examples below, which illustrate different intellectual actions and motivations – some virtuous, some not – can be adapted for use in upper- or lower-division courses in philosophy, and perhaps also for courses in the sciences and the humanities.[8] Each example asks students to identify the intellectual actions or motivations of the person in question, and evaluate whether someone with the intellectual virtues would do the same thing or have the same motives. Students should be reminded that the person in question can do what someone with the virtues would do, and even have the same motives, but still fail to fully possess the virtues.

Example 1: "Occam's Razor" from the Television Series House M.D. (2004)

House M.D., FOX television's award-winning medical drama, is a superb source of examples of intellectual actions. Each episode of the series dedicates several scenes to the process of diagnosis itself. The fictional Dr. House and his medical team are tasked with diagnosing patients whom no one else can diagnose. In so doing, they often perform actions that an intellectually virtuous person would perform. For instance, in the Season 1 episode "Occam's Razor," House and his team take on the case of Brandon, a college student who has low blood pressure, abdominal pain, fever, nausea, a cough, and a rash. Below is an excerpt from scene 2 "Deadly Treatment," in which House and his team begin the process of diagnosis.

> DR. HOUSE: "CBC was unremarkable, abdominal CT scan didn't show anything. So, people, differential diagnosis, what's wrong with her?"
>
> DR. CAMERON: "Him."
>
> DR. HOUSE: "Him, her, does it matter? Does anyone think it's a testicular problem? No. So, Chase?"
>
> DR. CHASE: "Yersinia infection?"
>
> DR. FOREMAN: "No, you wouldn't get the rash or cough. What about arthritis? Accompanying vasculitis causes nerve damage."
>
> DR. CAMERON: "No, it wouldn't cause the blood pressure problems. Allergy?"
>
> DR. CHASE: "The kid's got abdominal pain. Maybe carcinoid?"
>
> DR. FOREMAN: "No, but then you wouldn't get the . . ."
>
> DR. HOUSE: "Foreman, if you are going to list all the things it's not, it might be quicker to do it alphabetically. Absidia. Excellent. It doesn't account for any of these symptoms."
>
> DR. CAMERON: "No condition accounts for all these symptoms."
>
> DR. HOUSE: "Well, good, because I thought maybe he was sick, but apparently he's not. Who wants to draw up the discharge papers? Okay. Unless we control the blood pressure, he's going to start circling the drain before we can figure out what's wrong with him. Treat him for sepsis, broad spectrum antibiotics, and I want a cort stim test, and an echocardiogram."[9]

What intellectual actions did House and his team perform in this scene? What might their intellectual motivations be? What intellectual actions do you think a virtuous person would perform in this situation and why? What intellectual motivations would a virtuous person have in this situation and why? In other words, did House and his team perform intellectually virtuous actions and have intellectually virtuous motivations?

Example 2: Dr. Richard A. Muller's "The Conversion of a Climate Change Skeptic" (2012)

Public intellectuals and politicians sometimes sincerely change their minds about important issues. Though the media is apt to label such behavior as "flip-flopping," the person in question is often performing an act that an open-minded or intellectually courageous person would perform. Consider Dr. Richard A. Muller, a physicist at the University of California, Berkeley. Before 2012, Muller was critical of arguments for global warming, and doubted that global warming existed. On July 28, 2012, he published an opinion piece, "The Conversion of a Climate Change Skeptic," in the Op-Ed section of *The New York Times*, explaining why he had changed his mind. Below are excerpts from that piece.

> Call me a converted skeptic. Three years ago, I identified problems in previous climate studies that, in my mind, threw doubt on the very existence of global warming. Last year, following an intensive research effort by a dozen scientists, I concluded that global warming was real and that prior estimates of the rate of warming were correct . . .
>
> My total turnaround . . . is the result of careful and objective analysis by the Berkeley Earth Surface Temperature project. . . . Our results show that the average temperature of the earth's land has risen by two and a half degrees Fahrenheit over the past 250 years, including an increase of one and a half degrees over the most recent 50 years . . .
>
> Our Berkeley Earth approach used sophisticated statistical methods developed largely by our lead scientist, Robert Rohde, which allowed us to determine earth land temperature . . . further back in time. We carefully studied issues raised by skeptics: biases from urban heating (we duplicated our results using rural data alone), from data selection . . . from poor station quality (we separately analyzed good stations and poor ones), and from human intervention and data adjustment. . . . We demonstrate that none of these potentially troublesome effects unduly biased our conclusions.[10]

What intellectual actions did Muller, and his team of scientists, perform? What might their intellectual motivations have been? What intellectual actions do you think a virtuous person would have performed in this situation and why? What intellectual motivations would a virtuous person have had in this situation and why? Would an intellectually virtuous person have been in this situation to begin with? To sum up, did Muller and his team perform intellectually virtuous actions and have intellectually virtuous motivations?

Example 3: The Film Doubt (Miramax, 2008)

The brilliant 2008 film *Doubt*, directed and written by John Patrick Shanley, provides students with a wide range of examples of intellectual motivations, some of which a virtuous person would have, others of which she would not. *Doubt* is set in a Catholic School in the Bronx in 1964. Sister Aloysius, the seasoned principal of the school, suspects that Father Flynn, the parish priest, is having a sexual relationship with one of the boys at the school. That boy, Donald Miller, is a student in the class of Sister James – who is a new and inexperienced teacher at the school. During Sister James's class, Donald is called away for a private meeting with Father Flynn. When Donald returns, Sister James notices that he is behaving strangely and has the smell of alcohol on his breath. She reports this to Sister Aloysius. In scene 10, "Intolerance," the two sisters confront Father Flynn with this evidence. Below are excerpts from that scene.

> SISTER ALOYSIUS: "The boy acted strangely when he returned to class."
> FATHER FLYNN: "He did?"
> SISTER JAMES: "When he returned from the rectory, a little off, yes."
> SISTER ALOYSIUS: "Can you tell us why?"
> . . .
>
> SISTER ALOYSIUS: "What happened in the rectory?"
> FATHER FLYNN: "Happened? Nothing happened. I had a talk with the boy."
> . . .
>
> SISTER ALOYSIUS: "There was alcohol on his breath when he returned from his meeting with you."

FATHER FLYNN: "Alcohol?"
SISTER JAMES: "I did smell it on his breath."
. . .

Father Flynn: "Mr. McGuinn caught Donald drinking altar wine. When I found out I sent for him. There were tears. He begged not be removed from the altar boys. I took pity on him. I told him if no one else found out, I would let him stay on."
Sister James: "What a relief. That explains everything. Thanks be to God. Look sister it was all a mistake."
. . .

(Father Flynn departs.)
SISTER JAMES: "What a relief. He cleared it all up."
SISTER ALOYSIUS: "Do you believe him?"
SISTER JAMES: "Of course."
SISTER ALOYSIUS: "Isn't it that it is easier to believe him."
SISTER JAMES: "But we can corroborate his story with Mr. McGuinn."
SISTER ALOYSIUS: "Yes. These types of people are clever."
SISTER JAMES: "Well. I'm convinced."
SISTER ALOYSIUS: "You're not. You just want things to be resolved so that you can have simplicity back."
SISTER JAMES: "I want no further part of this."
SISTER ALOYSIUS: "I'll bring him down."
SISTER JAMES: "How can you be so sure that he is lying?"
SISTER ALOYSIUS: "Experience."
SISTER JAMES: "You just don't like him. You don't like it that he uses a ball point pen. You don't like it that he takes three lumps of sugar in his tea. You don't like it that he likes Frosty the Snow Man. And, you are letting that convince you of something terrible, just terrible . . ."[11]

What intellectual actions do Sister Aloysius and Sister James perform in this scene? What might their intellectual motivations be? Would an intellectually virtuous person have the same motivations in this situation? Why or why not? Throughout the film, Sister Aloysius demonstrates resistance to some kinds of change (e.g., changing the Christmas pageant, and the role of the school in the surrounding community), whereas Sister James demonstrates openness to these kinds of change. Is this relevant? Why or why not?

These examples provide students with opportunities to practice (1) *identifying* actions and motivations that are intellectually virtuous. But, to acquire intellectual virtues, it's not enough to merely know which actions and motivations are virtuous. Students must also have opportunities to practice (2) *performing* intellectually virtuous actions and *having* intellectually virtuous motivations. The classroom activity below, which can be conducted in small groups, gives students opportunities to practice these actions and motivations themselves. In the activity, students are given a philosophical problem; and are then asked to defend their answers, and to respond to others' answers. In so doing, they are asked to perform an action that an open-minded person would perform, and an action that an intellectually courageous person would perform. Here, too, students can be reminded that they need not fully possess the virtues in order to perform virtuous actions. They can also be reminded that an open-minded person considers reasonable alternatives to her own view, but need not change her view; and that an intellectually courageous person defends her view against objections, until she thinks that the objections succeed. In the version of the activity below, the philosophical problem is the famous "trolley problem."

Group Activity: The Trolley Problem

Imagine that you are standing on an overpass (flyover). Underneath the overpass runs a railway track. You see a runaway trolley hurtling down the track, coming in your direction. You are not in any danger, since you are on the overpass. But, unfortunately, there are five people tied to the railway track below, just beyond the overpass. They cannot move, and there is nobody else around who can help them. You are the only person who can prevent them from being killed by the runaway trolley. (This is an indisputable fact.) But, you are too far away to untie them. You know that the runaway trolley will stop if you drop a heavy weight in its path. As it happens, there is a very fat man also standing on the overpass. If you push the fat man off the overpass, then you will in fact stop the runaway trolley, and prevent it from killing the five people tied to the track. If you don't push the fat man off the overpass, then the runaway trolley will in fact kill the five people tied to the track. (These are indisputable facts.) There is no other way to prevent the trolley from killing them (e.g., you don't have time to reason with the fat man). What should you do? Should you push the fat man off the overpass?[12]

Answer the questions above, defend your answers (where appropriate), and respond to other students' answers (where appropriate). In so doing, try to perform: (1) at least one act that an open-minded person would perform; and (2) at least one act that an intellectually courageous person would perform. Once your group discussion is completed, briefly explain in writing two intellectual acts that you performed, and your motivations for performing them. Did you succeed in performing an act that an open-minded person would have performed? Did you succeed in performing an act that an intellectually courageous person would have performed? Did you fall short? What were your motivations? Was it difficult to try to be open-minded and intellectually courageous in the same conversation? Did these demands come into conflict?

Faculty can adapt the activity above to philosophical problems of their own choosing. One worry is that activities of this sort are contrived, and conducted in controlled circumstances. They instruct students to practice virtuous actions; thus their motives for doing so are not likely to be virtuous. Students are likely to perform virtuous actions because they have been asked to do so, not because they care about the truth for its own sake. A second problem is that these activities do not give students opportunities to practice sizing-up situations. They do not give students the opportunity to recognize for themselves when a situation calls for intellectually virtuous action. Instead, these activities provide "ready-made" circumstances that call for virtuous action.

The second problem is easier to solve than the first. Faculty can use a different kind of assignment to give students the chance to size-up situations for themselves. For instance, we can ask students to monitor classroom discussions, throughout the semester, for opportunities to practice intellectually virtuous actions. We might also consider a more radical assignment – incorporating a week of intellectually virtuous activity into our courses. During "Virtue Week," students would maintain a log of intellectually virtuous actions they performed. Those actions could be performed inside or outside the classroom – in writing papers, giving presentations, conducting research, evaluating the media, or in conversations with colleagues at work, or with their friends or families – thus encouraging students to recognize opportunities for intellectually virtuous action. Students would then complete the following assignment.

Virtue Week Assignment

Review your log. Identify two types of intellectually virtuous acts – for example, open-minded acts, intellectually courageous acts, etc. – that you performed repeatedly. Recall that you can perform, for example, open-minded acts – you can do what an open-minded person would do – even if you don't fully possess the virtue of open-mindedness. Write a three-page paper in which you describe: (1) two instances of each of these two types of acts (e.g., two examples of open-minded acts that you performed, and two examples of intellectually courageous acts that you performed); and (2) an intellectual act that you performed that fell short of a virtuous act. Be sure to explain your motivations for performing each of these five acts.[13]

Granted, the Virtue Week assignment still has the problem of being contrived. Students often report that they performed virtuous acts because the assignment required them to, or because they wanted to get a good grade, not because they cared about getting the truth for its own sake. Within the confines of a structured class, it may be difficult to provide students with opportunities to practice intrinsic motivations, like caring about the truth for its sake. But faculty can provide students with opportunities to engage in discussion, and write papers, that do not affect their grades. If we don't do this in our own courses, we can at least foster an environment in which students exchange ideas outside class. For instance, we can support an environment that enables students to attend talks, participate in Philosophy Clubs, or present their papers to one another or to student groups on campus. None of these activities is directly tied to pleasing faculty or getting grades. We might also consider Deci et al.'s conclusion that positive verbal feedback can foster the intrinsic motivation for truth. Many faculty spontaneously provide such feedback. In so doing, we may already be helping our students develop the intrinsic motivation for truth.

Of course, none of the strategies above is guaranteed to succeed. Nor will these strategies turn us, or our students, into intellectually virtuous people in a single semester. But, what these strategies can do is help our students *begin* to develop intellectual virtues. Granted, acquiring the dispositions of action and motivation that are needed for the virtues won't be easy. It will require something like the process of habituation described above. As faculty, we can help our students get started on this process. We can help our students understand what the intellectual virtues are, and why they are valuable. We can also expose our students to exemplars, or near exemplars, of intellectual virtue – by exposing them to fictional characters like Dr. House, and to a range of excellent thinkers in assigned readings. Finally, we can provide them with opportunities to practice: (1) *identifying* intellectually virtuous actions and motivations; and (2) *performing* intellectually virtuous actions and *having* intellectually virtuous motivations themselves. Combining all of these efforts, we can realistically expect our students to make some progress in developing intellectual virtues, even in a single semester. We have two further reasons to be hopeful. First, if we embrace weak situationism and endorse nearly global virtues, then the virtues will be a bit less daunting and slightly easier to acquire than we might have initially thought. Second, those of us who fall short of fully possessing the nearly global virtues can still make progress toward *enkrateia*, and toward reducing our number of blind spots. All this means that although the process described above is not perfect, it is still likely to get us closer to possessing intellectual virtue.[14]

Notes

1 What Are the Virtues?

1 See the HBO film *Iron-Jawed Angels* (2004).

2 Granted, hard-wired qualities like reliable memory are not personal, nor are they qualities for which one can be praised. As Jason Baehr insightfully puts the point, impersonal qualities like a reliable memory do not contribute to one's "personal intellectual worth" (see his brilliant book *The Inquiring Mind*, p. 92). But, contributing to one's personal intellectual worth isn't the only way for a quality to be an intellectual virtue (though it is one way – see section 1.2.2 below). Qualities like reliable memory are intellectual virtues because they enable us to produce intellectual goods: they make us excellent by enabling us to produce true beliefs and knowledge (see section 1.2.1 below). Accordingly, there will be intellectual virtues (excellences) that do not contribute to one's personal intellectual worth. Baehr also allows for this possibility (2011: 124). To put the same point differently, I am using the phrase "quality that makes one an excellent person" to encompass *both*: qualities that make one excellent *as* a person or *qua* person – personal qualities (see section 1.2.2); *and* qualities that make one, who is a person, excellent – even when these latter qualities are impersonal (see section 1.2.1).

3 See Hume 1966/1751: 166. In his *Dialogues Concerning Natural Religion* (1947/1779), Hume argues against the notion of an omnipotent, omniscient, omnibenevolent God.

4 Michael Slote uses a similar example. See Slote 2001: 26.

5   That is, one need not have good motives *unless* the good ends or effects are themselves defined so as to require good motives. See the remarks on Plato and Aristotle below.

6   To know what is good, on Plato's view, one must gain access to the form of the good. See *Republic*, Books VI and VII.

7   See Sosa 2003; and Sosa 2007, Lecture 4.

8   Sosa (1991 and 2007) focuses on intellectual virtues that are hard-wired capacities and acquired skills. Sosa has not focused on intellectual virtues that are character traits. But he does not preclude character traits from being intellectual virtues. In fact, one of Sosa's more recent works, "Epistemic Agency" (2011) indicates a shift toward addressing character traits as intellectual virtues.

9   Michael Slote uses a similar example in his book *Moral Sentimentalism* (2010: 134).

10   But, unlike Hume, Slote is not a consequentialist about virtue.

2   Ends Matter: Virtues Attain Good Ends or Effects

1   Plato and Aristotle think that children learn to care about people for their own sakes by first caring about external rewards.

2   See Watson 1968; Roberts and Wood 2007: 294–298.

3   Recall that according to the first key concept of virtue, virtues need not involve internal features like emotions, desires, or motives. Plato and Aristotle think that virtues *do* involve these internal features because they define human function as partly internal. To excel at rational activity, ruling oneself, and/or living well, one must line up one's desires and motives with the dictates of reason.

4   Does Rosalind Hursthouse also employ the first key concept of virtue? In *On Virtue Ethics*, she does employ a teleological notion of the good. But, she does *not* employ a teleological notion of virtue. In Chapters 4–7, she explicitly argues that virtues are character traits that require acting from (the right) reasons and motives. So, she endorses the second key concept of virtue, not the first. Granted, she does use her teleological notion of the good as a *second* test for which traits count as virtues. To count as a virtue, on her view, a trait must foster our human functions. But, to even get to this second test, a trait must have already passed Hursthouse's *first* test for virtue: it must be a character trait that involves acting from (the right)

reasons and motives (1999: 207–209). Hursthouse does *not* think that any old quality that fosters our ends counts as a virtue. The only qualities that even make it to the second test are qualities like impersonal benevolence and temperance, which pass the first test. Thus, Hursthouse points out that since vegetarianism isn't even a character trait, we need not consider whether it fosters our human functions (1999: 227). Many thanks to Christine Swanton for raising this thoughtful worry.

5   Relatedly, suppose that a tiger has "virtues" that enable it to be a good specimen of its kind. Here, too, the teleological notion of virtue only tells us that the tiger has qualities that enable it to attain its end. It does not tell us whether the end, or the qualities that attain it, are morally good or bad. To assume that these qualities are morally good would be to commit the naturalistic fallacy – to infer a moral "ought" from a biological "is." Hursthouse addresses this issue in *On Virtue Ethics*, Ch. 10.

6   Contingent truths are actually true, but could have been false. It is contingently true that in 2013, Obama was the President of the United States. In contrast, necessary truths cannot possibly be false. It is necessarily true that $1 + 1 = 2$.

7   Here, Sosa cites Plato's *Republic*, 352. See also Sosa 2009: 187.

8   The intuition that underlies much contemporary epistemology is that we should start by analyzing relatively straightforward cases of contingent knowledge; e.g., how do we know that "The car is red"? Providing answers in the straightforward cases will help us analyze more complicated cases of contingent knowledge – e.g., how we know what to do.

9   Sosa 1991: 139. See also Battaly 2008.

10   But, see Sosa 2011. Sosa may ultimately argue that although intellectual virtues like memory and vision do not require desire or action, intellectual virtues that are character traits do.

11   Sosa (2009) distinguishes between animal knowledge, like visual knowledge, which we share with animals; and reflective knowledge, which is unique to us. He addresses understanding in the context of reflective knowledge.

12   See also Driver's example of the Mutors (2001: 55–56). Some of the Mutors have bad motives – they want to beat children who are exactly 5.57 years old. It turns out that in their world, doing so dramatically increases the life expectancy of those children, and so produces overall social benefits. But, that is not their motive for doing it. Thus, they have virtues, despite their obviously bad motives.

13   On Gage, see Damasio 1994.

14 See also Slote 2001; Montmarquet 1993.
15 Driver 2001: 69.
16 There is more than one kind of luck: luck in the outcomes of one's actions, luck in one's environment, and luck in the development of one's character. See Nagel 1979: Ch. 3; Nelkin 2013. Annas's and Foot's accounts insulate virtue from bad luck in the outcomes of one's actions, and the bad luck of landing in an inhospitable environment. But, they arguably don't insulate virtue from bad constitutive luck. In other words, bad luck in the development of one's character – e.g., lack of access to exemplars – can still prevent one from having the virtues. The relations between the different kinds of luck are complicated: for instance, bad luck in one's environment can also produce constitutive bad luck. Thanks to Neera Badhwar for raising this important point.

3   Motives Matter: Virtues Require Good Motives

1 See Roberts and Wood's excellent analysis (2007: 294–297).
2 These are the words of Michael Eisen, a geneticist, who is quoted in Hiltzik 2013.
3 Of course, she must also have all the other good psychological states and dispositions of actions needed for these virtues, including additional motives and values, appropriate emotions, and knowledge.
4 But, Aristotle does acknowledge that we may acquire the virtues in different ways. For example, if I tend toward cowardice, but you tend toward rashness, then in order to acquire the virtue of courage, I may initially need to overcompensate by performing some rash actions, whereas you may need to perform some cowardly actions.
5 Technically, Aristotle claims that it is determined by the "man" of practical wisdom. Aristotle was a sexist; and his views about women are flat-out false.
6 Recall that Aristotle also endorses the first key concept of virtue, whereby virtues are qualities that enable us to live well. Aristotle may ultimately combine the first key concept with the second key concept. That is, he may ultimately think that moral virtues are character traits that require choice, *and* enable us to live well. This may help explain why he thinks that the virtues are constitutively (and often instrumentally) valuable.

7   For Hursthouse, as for Aristotle, we must also have appropriate emotions (e.g., we must be angered and disappointed by dishonesty), and appropriate perceptions (e.g., we must notice occasions for honesty).

8   She also thinks that virtue requires appropriate emotions.

9   Hursthouse doesn't think these conditions are sufficient. The honest person must also have appropriate emotions and perceptions.

10 Aristotle seems to think that the virtue of magnificence (NE. IV.2) requires external success.

11 But, there is also some reason to think that Hursthouse could fall in the motives-actions-and-ends camp. After all, she thinks that bad luck in the way we are brought up as children can prevent us from having virtues. Accordingly, we might expect her to draw a similar conclusion about the bad luck that thwarts our efforts to produce good ends or effects. Recall that there are different kinds of luck – luck in the outcomes of one's actions, luck in one's environment, and luck in the development of one's character – and that the relations between them are complicated. See Chapter 2, note 16.

12 For examples of scientists motivated by fame, see Hiltzik 2013.

13 We can't derive "warm" motives like caring from the motive of inner strength. And, even if we could, Slote thinks we shouldn't, since motives like caring are basic (rather than derivative) moral values (2001: 20–23).

14 We could introduce a similar view with respect to the first key concept of virtue. To some extent, Sosa's view already does that: he claims that demon-victims have intellectual virtues relative to our world, but do not have intellectual virtues relative to their demon-world.

15 NE.1097b2-3; Zagzebski 1996: 203–207.

16 A notable exception is Hurka 2001. Thanks to an anonymous referee for raising this point.

4   Vice and Failures of Virtue

1   Driver 2001: 57.

2   Sosa does not often use the term "vice," but he does use the phrase "flawed epistemic character" (1991: 241).

3   See Sosa 1991: 289; 2007: 22; Battaly 2014c.

4   Chapters 1 and 2 sometimes treat vice as a failure to get the good, rather than a disposition to get the bad.

5   For an insightful analysis of why Hitler was blameworthy for his false beliefs, see Montmarquet 1993.

6   http://cardinalrogermahonyblogsla.blogspot.com/2013/02/historical-evolution-of-dealing-with.html

7   I am grateful to an anonymous referee for raising this point.

8   For objections, see Howard Curzer's paper "Good People with Bad Principles," presented at the Pacific Meeting of the American Philosophical Association, San Francisco, March 28, 2013.

9   Baehr employs an epistemically internalist reading of this vice; whereas the above employs an epistemically externalist reading.

10 But, see Swanton 2003: 24.

5 Virtue, Right Action, and Knowledge

1   Zagzebski argues that acts of intellectual virtue, which themselves entail truth, are necessary and sufficient for knowledge.

2   Swanton (2003) and Slote (2001) offer different theories of right action. See also Van Zyl 2011; Russell 2009.

3   There is a second reason for thinking that virtuous acts are not sufficient for right acts. If one thinks that virtues like courage can be had by otherwise vicious people (e.g., Hitler), then doing what a courageous person would characteristically do will not be sufficient for performing a right act. See Zagzebski 1996: 95. To perform a right act, one must not only have the virtue of courage, one must have other virtues like benevolence, justice, etc.

4   Some moral situations do not involve dilemmas at all. See Swanton 2003: 69–70.

5   See van Zyl's excellent 2011.

6   Likewise, there are circumstances in which a woman who gets pregnant after intentionally having sex should have an abortion, even though doing so is not right. See Hursthouse 1997: 235.

7   Arguably, a virtuous person would tell the truth even if she had the option to say nothing.

8   Even the Chronic Liar can be in this situation. When he is, he won't perform a right act unless he does what a virtuous person would do (i.e., tell the truth). It is just that the Chronic Liar can also be in situations that the virtuous person cannot be in; for example, he can be in the situation of "needing to log his progress in telling the truth."

9 Likewise, forcing girls into sexual slavery may be wrong because it violates their rights, not because it is what a vicious person would do.

10 See Crisp 2010: 21–24.

11 She thinks acts of intellectual virtue, which by definition entail true beliefs, are sufficient for knowledge.

12 To perform an act of intellectual courage, one must be motivated to (a) get truth and (b) stand up for one's beliefs. And, on this occasion, one must do what an intellectually courageous person would do, get a true belief, and get a true belief because of one's action and motivation.

13 If we fully possess the virtue of open-mindedness, then we consistently perform acts of open-mindedness.

14 The first key concept of intellectual virtue is much better than the second key concept at analyzing low-grade knowledge. Battaly 2008: 655–656.

15 You deduce that since Austin owns a Mac, someone in Austin's Intro to Philosophy class owns a Mac. You are not in Austin's Philosophy class, nor do you have knowledge of who is, nor do you have knowledge of Mac sales or of the percentage of students who own Macs, etc.

16 This example is adapted from Baehr 2006: 487–488. See also Battaly 2008.

17 I am grateful to an anonymous referee for suggesting this reply.

18 Zagzebski makes some headway on this issue in her 1996: 246–253.

19 At least he doesn't care about truth for its own sake. For Zagzebski's replies, see her 1996: 315–316.

20 See Watson 1968: 157–163; Battaly 2010: 379; Roberts and Wood 2007: 145, 294–296.

21 For an excellent recent account of testimony, see Fricker 2007.

22 So, perhaps, we should think of high-grade knowledge as requiring active inquiry on the part of some member of our epistemic community, even if it does not require active inquiry on the part of every agent who possesses it.

6 Virtue and Living Well

1 See Cicero 1914, 1942; Epictetus 1995; Annas 2011, 2002.

2 Exceptions include Haybron 2008; Cahn 2004; and Hursthouse 1999: 173. Snow defends the claim that virtue is necessary for living well against counterexamples; see her excellent 2008.

3   These conclusions clearly apply to the motives-actions-no-ends variety of the second key concept of virtue. Whether they also apply to the motives-actions-and ends variety, and to the first key concept of virtue, will depend on the ends and effects that those virtues reliably produce. If those virtues reliably produce ends and effects that benefit other people but not the virtuous agent herself, then the conclusions above still apply.

4   On the distinction between good and good for, see Crisp 2013; Haybron 2008: 36–38.

5   As soon as a life gets worse, it is no longer the best life.

6   This does *not* mean that all kinds of lives – e.g., even that of an executioner – will be good for agents.

7   One of the things that is so insidious about slavery, and sex trafficking, is that they can change people's desires.

8   A virtuous person knows what she can control and what she can't. She also does her best, given the circumstances.

9   They agree that the virtues are necessary for living well, even if they disagree with Aristotle about whether the virtues are sufficient for living well.

10   The Stoics think that we can use *any* objects well or badly; and that things like wealth and health do not do us any good unless we have the virtues. But, this is false: having enough wealth to prevent ourselves from starving – to put us over the threshold – does us good. The same can be said of freedom and health.

7   How Can We Acquire the Virtues?

1   See also Battaly 2006; Kotzee 2014; and Jason Baehr's Intellectual Virtues & Education Project: http://intellectualvirtues. org/

2   Thanks to Jason Baehr for raising this point.

3   See Deci et al. 2001.

4   The account of habituation above is at least partly correct. There is ample evidence that extrinsic motivation can get us to perform and practice virtuous acts. Extrinsic motivation may even enable us to overcome weakness of will. See Baumeister and Tierney 2011: 34, 152–154.

5   See also Battaly 2014b.

6   See also Russell's analysis (2012: 123) of Arius Didymus, a Stoic who indexed virtues to conditions.

7   See also Flanagan 1991, 2009; Badhwar 2014; Battaly 2014b.

8 I have used the examples, activities, and assignments below in upper-division courses in epistemology, and lower-division courses in logic.

9 "Occam's Razor" originally aired on Fox on November 30, 2004.

10 http://www.nytimes.com/2012/07/30/opinion/the-conversion -of-a-climate-change-skeptic.html?_r=0

11 *Doubt* was released by Miramax on December 25, 2008.

12 For Judith Jarvis Thomson's original fat man example, see her 1985: 1409. Philippa Foot (1967) introduced the original version of the trolley problem.

13 See Battaly 2006: 217.

14 I am grateful to the Spencer Foundation, and to Cal State Fullerton, for providing me with grants that supported the research for Chapter 7.

References

Adams, Katherine H. and Michael L. Keene. 2008. *Alice Paul and the American Suffrage Campaign*. Chicago: University of Illinois Press.

Adams, Robert. 2006. *A Theory of Virtue*. New York: Oxford University Press.

Annas, Julia. 2002. "Should Virtue Make you Happy?" *Apeiron* 35(4): 1–19.

Annas, Julia. 2003. "The Structure of Virtue." In *Intellectual Virtue*, eds. Michael DePaul and Linda Zagzebski. New York: Oxford University Press, pp. 15–33.

Annas, Julia. 2011. *Intelligent Virtue*. New York: Oxford University Press.

Aristotle. 1984. *Nicomachean Ethics*. In *The Complete Works of Aristotle*, vol. 2, ed. Jonathan Barnes. Princeton: Princeton University Press.

Aristotle. 1998. *The Nicomachean Ethics*. Trans. David Ross. New York: Oxford University Press.

Asch, Solomon E. 1952. *Social Psychology*. Englewood Cliffs, NJ: Prentice-Hall.

Badhwar, Neera. 2014. *Well-Being: Happiness in a Worthwhile Life*. Oxford: Oxford University Press.

Baehr, Jason. 2006. "Character in Epistemology." *Philosophical Studies* 128: 479–514.

Baehr, Jason. 2010. "Epistemic Malevolence." *Metaphilosophy* 41: 189–213.

Baehr, Jason. 2011. *The Inquiring Mind: On Intellectual Virtues and Virtue Epistemology*. Oxford: Oxford University Press.

Battaly, Heather. 2001. "Thin Concepts to the Rescue." In *Virtue Epistemology*, eds. Abrol Fairweather and Linda Zagzebski. Oxford: Oxford University Press, pp. 98–116.

Battaly, Heather. 2006. "Teaching Intellectual Virtues." *Teaching Philosophy* 29(3): 191–222.

Battaly, Heather. 2007. "Intellectual Virtue and Knowing One's Sexual Orientation." In *Sex and Ethics*, ed. Raja Halwani. New York: Palgrave Macmillan, pp. 149–161.

Battaly, Heather. 2008. "Virtue Epistemology." *Philosophy Compass* 3(4): 639–663.

Battaly, Heather. 2010a. "Epistemic Self-Indulgence." *Metaphilosophy* 41: 214–234.

Battaly, Heather. 2010b. "Attacking Character: Ad Hominem Argument and Virtue Epistemology." *Informal Logic* 30(4): 361–390.

Battaly, Heather. 2014a. "Intellectual Virtues." In *The Handbook of Virtue Ethics*, ed. Stan Van Hooft. Durham: Acumen, pp. 177–187.

Battaly, Heather. 2014b. "Acquiring Epistemic Virtue: Emotions, Situations, and Education." In *Naturalizing Epistemic Virtue*, eds. Abrol Fairweather and Owen Flanagan. Cambridge: Cambridge University Press, pp. 175–196.

Battaly, Heather. 2014c. "Varieties of Epistemic Vice." In *The Ethics of Belief*, eds. Jon Matheson and Rico Vitz. Oxford University Press.

Baumeister, Roy F. and John Tierney. 2011. *Willpower*. New York: Penguin Press.

Cahn, Steven M. 2004. "The Happy Immoralist." *Journal of Social Philosophy* 35(1): 1.

Cicero. 1914. *De Finibus*. Trans. H. Rackham. Cambridge, MA: Harvard University Press.

Cicero. 1942. *Stoic Paradoxes*. Trans. H. Rackham. Cambridge, MA: Harvard University Press.

Crisp, Roger. 2010. "Virtue Ethics and Virtue Epistemology." *Metaphilosophy* 41: 22–40.

Crisp, Roger. 2013. "Well-Being." In *The Stanford Encyclopedia of Philosophy*, ed. Edward N. Zalta. http://plato.stanford.edu/entries/well-being/

Damasio, Antonio. 1994. *Descartes' Error*. New York: HarperCollins.

Darley, John M. and C. Daniel Batson. 1973. "From Jerusalem to Jericho." *Journal of Personality and Social Psychology* 27(1): 100–108.

Deci, Edward L., Richard Koestner, and Richard M. Ryan. 2001. "Extrinsic Rewards and Intrintic Motivation in Education:

Reconsidered Once Again." *Review of Educational Research* 71: 1–27.

Doris, John M. 2002. *Lack of Character*. Cambridge: Cambridge University Press.

Driver, Julia. 2001. *Uneasy Virtue*. New York: Cambridge University Press.

Ekman, Paul. 2009. *Telling Lies*, 3rd edn. New York: W. W. Norton & Co.

Eliot, George. 1984[1874]. *Middlemarch*. New York: Modern Library.

Ellis, Bret Easton. 1991. *American Psycho*. New York: Vintage.

Epictetus. 1995. *The Discourses*, ed. C. Gill. Rutland, VT: Everyman.

Flanagan, Owen. 1991. *Varieties of Moral Personality*. Cambridge, MA: Harvard University Press.

Flanagan, Owen. 2009. "Moral Science? Still Metaphysical After All These Years." In *Personality, Identity and Character*, eds. Darcia Narvaez and Daniel K. Lapsley. New York: Cambridge University Press, pp. 59–78.

Foot, Philippa. 1967. "The Problem of Abortion and the Doctrine of Double Effect." *Oxford Review* 5: 5–15.

Foot, Philippa. 1997. "Virtues and Vices." In *Virtue Ethics*, eds. Roger Crisp and Michael Slote. Oxford: Oxford University Press, pp. 163–177.

Fricker, Miranda. 2007. *Epistemic Injustice*. Oxford University Press.

Friedman, Marilyn. 2009. "Feminist Virtue Ethics, Happiness, and Moral Luck." *Hypatia* 24: 29–40.

Gettier, Edmund. 1963. "Is True Justified Belief Knowledge?" *Analysis* 23(6): 121–123.

Harman, Gilbert. 1999. "Moral Philosophy Meets Social Psychology." *Proceedings of the Aristotelian Society* 99: 315–331.

Haybron, Daniel M. 2008. *The Pursuit of Unhappiness*. New York: Oxford University Press.

Hiltzik, Michael. 2013. "Science Has Lost its Way, at a Big Cost to Humanity." *Los Angeles Times*, Oct. 27, 2013.

Hume, David. 1947[1779]. *Dialogues Concerning Natural Religion*, 2nd edn. Ed. N. Kemp Smith. Edinburgh: Nelson & Sons.

Hume, David. 1966[1751]. *An Enquiry Concerning the Principles of Morals*. La Salle, IL: Open Court. 1978.

Hume, David. 1978[1738]. *A Treatise of Human Nature*, 2nd edn. Ed. L. A. Selby-Bigge. Oxford: Oxford University Press.

Hurka, Thomas. 2001. *Virtue, Vice, and Value*. New York: Oxford University Press.

Hursthouse, Rosalind. 1997. "Virtue Theory and Abortion." In *Virtue Ethics*, eds. Roger Crisp and Michael Slote. Oxford: Oxford University Press, pp. 217–238.

Hursthouse, Rosalind. 1999. *On Virtue Ethics*. Oxford: Oxford University Press.

Johnson, Robert. 2003. "Virtue and Right." *Ethics* 113: 810–834.

Kim, Victoria, Ashley Powers, and Harriet Ryan. 2013. "L.A. Church Leaders Sought to Hide Sex Abuse Cases from Authorities." *Los Angeles Times*, Jan. 21, 2013.

Kotzee, Ben, ed. 2014. *Education and the Growth of Knowledge*. Oxford: Wiley-Blackwell.

Kristof, Nicholas D. and Sheryl WuDunn. 2009. *Half the Sky*. New York: Knopf.

Lynch, Michael P. 1998. *Truth in Context*. Cambridge, MA: The MIT Press.

Milgram, Stanley. 1974. *Obedience to Authority*. New York: Harper and Row.

Montmarquet, James A. 1993. *Epistemic Virtue and Doxastic Responsibility*. Lanham, MD: Rowman & Littlefield.

Muller, Richard A. 2012. "The Conversion of a Climate Change Skeptic." *The New York Times*, July 28, 2012.

Nagel, Thomas. 1979. *Mortal Questions*. New York: Cambridge University Press.

Nelkin, Dana K. 2013. "Moral Luck." In *The Stanford Encyclopedia of Philosophy*, ed. Edward N. Zalta. http://plato.stanford.edu/entries/moral-luck/.

Nozick, Robert. 1977. *Anarchy, State, and Utopia*. New York: Basic Books.

Plato. 1961. *Euthydemus*. In *The Collected Dialogues of Plato*, ed. Edith Hamilton and Huntington Cairns. Princeton: Princeton University Press.

Plato. 1961. *Protagoras*. In *The Collected Dialogues of Plato*, ed. Edith Hamilton and Huntington Cairns. Princeton: Princeton University Press.

Plato. 1992. *Republic*. Trans. G. M. A. Grube. Indianapolis, IN: Hackett Publishing Company.

Roberts, Robert C. 1987. "Will Power and the Virtues." In *The Virtues*, eds. Robert B. Kruschwitz and Robert C. Roberts. Belmont, CA: Wadsworth Publishing, pp. 122–136.

Roberts, Robert C. and W. Jay Wood. 2007. *Intellectual Virtues: An Essay in Regulative Epistemology*. Oxford: Oxford University Press.

Rowling, J. K. 1997. *Harry Potter and the Sorcerer's Stone*. New York: Scholastic Inc.

Rowling, J. K. 1998. *Harry Potter and the Chamber of Secrets*. New York: Scholastic Inc.

Rowling, J. K. 1999. *Harry Potter and the Prisoner of Azkaban*. New York: Scholastic Inc.

Russell, Daniel C. 2009. *Practical Intelligence and the Virtues*. Oxford: Oxford University Press.

Russell, Daniel C. 2012. *Happiness for Humans*. New York: Oxford University Press.

Sherman, Nancy. 1989. *The Fabric of Character*. Oxford: Clarendon Press.

Slote, Michael. 2001. *Morals from Motives*. Oxford: Oxford University Press.

Slote, Michael. 2010. *Moral Sentimentalism*. New York: Oxford University Press.

Snow, Nancy E. 2008. "Virtue and Flourishing." *Journal of Social Philosophy* 39(2): 225–245.

Sosa, Ernest. 1991. *Knowledge in Perspective*. New York: Cambridge University Press.

Sosa, Ernest. 2003. "The Place of Truth in Epistemology." In *Intellectual Virtue*, eds. Michael DePaul and Linda Zagzebski. New York: Oxford University Press, pp. 155–179.

Sosa, Ernest. 2007. *A Virtue Epistemology*. Oxford: Oxford University Press.

Sosa, Ernest. 2009. *Reflective Knowledge*. Oxford: Oxford University Press.

Sosa, Ernest. 2011. "Epistemic Agency." In *Knowing Full Well*. Princeton: Princeton University Press, pp. 14–34.

Stocker, Michael. 1979. "Desiring the Bad." *Journal of Philosophy* 76: 738–753.

Styron, William. 1979. *Sophie's Choice*. New York: Vintage Books.

Swanton, Christine. 2003. *Virtue Ethics: A Pluralistic View*. New York: Oxford University Press.

Thomson, Judith Jarvis. 1985. "The Trolley Problem." *Yale Law Journal* 94(6): 1395–1415.

Van Zyl, Liezl. 2011. "Qualified Agent Virtue Ethics." *South African Journal of Philosophy* 30(2): 219–228.

Watson, James D. 1968. *The Double Helix*. New York: Touchstone.

Yousafzai, Malala (with Christina Lamb). 2013. *I Am Malala*. New York: Little, Brown, and Co.

Zagzebski, Linda Trinkaus. 1996. *Virtues of the Mind: An Inquiry into the Nature of Virtue and the Ethical Foundations of Knowledge*. Cambridge: Cambridge University Press.

Index